ART CURRICULUM
ACTIVITIES KITS
Intermediate Level

Written and illustrated

by

Barbara McNally Reuther

and

Diane Enemark Fogler

PARKER PUBLISHING COMPANY
West Nyack, New York 10995

Library of Congress Cataloging-in-Publication Data

Reuther, Barbara McNally.
  Art curriculum activities kits, intermediate level
Barbara McNally Reuther, Diane Enemark Fogler.
    p.   cm.
  ISBN 0-13-047184-4
  1. Art—Study and teaching (Elementary)—United States.   2. Art—
Study and teaching (Secondary)—United States.   3. Activity
programs in education—United States.   I. Fogler, Diane Enemark.
II. Title.
N362.R48   1988   87-38480
707'.1273—dc19   CIP

ISBN 0-13-047184-4

PARKER PUBLISHING COMPANY
BUSINESS & PROFESSIONAL DIVISION
A division of Simon & Schuster
West Nyack, New York 10995

About the Authors

Author/illustrator Barbara McNally Reuther, B.A. Art, has taught art at the elementary level for over seven years in the Rockaway Township School District in New Jersey. Mrs. Reuther has initiated and developed enrichment classes for students gifted in the visual arts and has also worked extensively in the areas of curriculum development and art assessment.

Author Diane Enemark Fogler, M.A. Art, has taught art at the elementary, junior, and senior high school levels for more than twenty years. She currently teaches art at the elementary level and serves as art coordinator for the Rockaway Township School District in New Jersey. Mrs. Fogler has conducted in-service art workshops for classroom teachers and has also worked extensively with gifted students in an art enrichment program. She has served as art director at various day camps and recreation centers and has also written her district's elementary art curriculum as well as several articles for *School Arts Magazine*.

Dedication

To my husband, Charlie,
for his enthusiastic support and encouragement
and to my parents,
the most creative teachers I know.

B.M.R.

To the children I have taught,
who made each day
a challenge and an adventure.

D.E.F.

Acknowledgments

We wish to thank Win Huppuch for the chance he offered us to do this book, and Ann Leuthner for her editorial assistance and reassuring support throughout.

About the Art Curriculum Activities Kits

Our objective in creating these *Art Curriculum Activities Kits* was to provide teachers with new, stimulating, creative art activities that teach basic art concepts and skills and that meet the curricular needs of students at various age and skill levels. Within two volumes, the primary and intermediate levels, teachers will find a comprehensive art curriculum for students in grades 1–8, presented in 150 easy-to-use art lessons. These lessons are carefully designed for the skills sequentially developed between grades 1 and 8. Each lesson has its own full-page illustration and step-by-step student-level directions.

Each book contains three skill levels, which increase in complexity. Within each level the individual lessons are categorized by media. These include drawing, painting, weaving, color and design, ceramics, paper crafts, printmaking and crafts. All of the lessons presented make use of inexpensive and commonly available materials and have been classroom tested by the authors and proven to be highly successful.

The organized format and clear graphic presentation of each book make it possible for the teacher with little or no previous art training to teach these lessons successfully. The art specialist will find that these books provide a valuable curricular guide and ability-level source book.

One of the most important features of our presentation is the skill level sequence. The examples presented below are included to give an overview of the developmental process from Level 1 to Level 6. At each level new skills and media are introduced, while previously acquired skills and techniques are reinforced.

In addition, you'll find detailed, full-page illustrations and easy to-use directions.

WEAVING

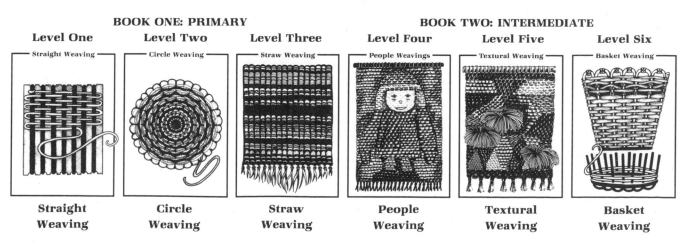

BOOK ONE: PRIMARY			BOOK TWO: INTERMEDIATE		
Level One	Level Two	Level Three	Level Four	Level Five	Level Six
Straight Weaving	Circle Weaving	Straw Weaving	People Weavings	Textural Weaving	Basket Weaving
Straight Weaving	Circle Weaving	Straw Weaving	People Weaving	Textural Weaving	Basket Weaving

SPECIAL FEATURES OF THIS BOOK

- A comprehensive, sequential art curriculum designed for more advanced levels, or approximately for grades 5–8, depending on individual ability levels.

- Innovative activities in eight different art media which teach basic and advanced art skills and concepts.

- Seventy-five lessons provided with full-page illustrations for each. These illustrations may be used for demonstration purposes or to provide helpful ideas on what to add to each project.

- Smaller "how-to" illustrations are included in the step-by-step directions for ease of use. Direction sheets may also be reproduced and distributed to students for group or independent use.

- Each art concept is built upon another art concept, thus providing a strong foundation for all future art skills.

- Each individual lesson contains a list of materials which makes it easy to see-at-a-glance what is needed for each project.

- Easy-to-use, comprehensive step-by-step directions are provided for each lesson.

- The Table of Contents presents the material in two convenient forms: (1) Activities are categorized by media so that lessons can quickly be found in any given subject area, and (2) media categories are divided into three skill levels so that lessons are easily located for students with varying art skills.

- All of the activities in this book have been classroom tested and proven successful.

- This book explores and introduces a wide variety of art forms and media, which help to build sequential art skills while reinforcing skills previously used. And—each activity is fun and unique—so enjoy!

Contents

About These Kits
Special Features
Focus Areas/Skills Charts

Color and Design

SECTION III

SECTION IV

Ceramics

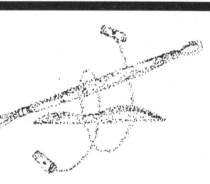

SECTION V

Paper Crafts

Focus Areas

	line	shape	value	color	texture	perspective & proportion	pattern & composition	cultural enrichment	creative thinking
Section I: Drawing									
I-1 Self-Portrait	•	•				•		•	•
I-2 Body Portraits	•	•		•		•		•	•
I-3 Castle Drawings		•				•	•	•	•
I-4 Royal Portrait	•	•		•		•		•	•
I-5 Motivational Drawings			•		•		•		•
I-6 Hide and Seek	•	•	•		•	•	•		•
I-7 Zoo Murals		•		•	•	•			•
I-8 Scratchboards	•		•		•		•		•
I-9 Imagination Machines	•	•				•	•		•
Section II: Painting									
II-1 Giant Paper Ice Cream Cones	•	•		•			•		•
II-2 Pussy Willows	•	•	•	•	•	•			•
II-3 Sidewalk Paintings	•	•		•		•		•	•
II-4 Painted Skeletons	•	•				•		•	•
II-5 Big Bad Bug Painting	•	•		•	•	•	•		•
II-6 Painted Turkeys	•	•		•	•	•	•		•
II-7 Glowing Fish	•	•	•	•		•	•		•
II-8 Fabric Painting	•	•	•	•			•	•	•
Section III: Color and Design									
III-1 Letter Pictures	•	•					•		•
III-2 Horizontal and Vertical Designs	•		•	•			•		•
III-3 Crayon Picture Puzzles	•	•	•	•		•	•		•
III-4 Photograms	•	•	•				•		•
III-5 All-Over Patterns	•	•	•				•		•
III-6 One Shape Only	•	•	•				•		•
III-7 Crayon Fireworks	•	•	•	•			•		•
III-8 Pattern Birds	•	•		•	•	•			•
III-9 Line Art	•		•				•		•
III-10 Word Pictures	•	•	•	•			•		•
III-11 Sunglasses		•		•			•		•
III-12 Collage Portraits	•	•		•	•	•	•	•	•
III-13 Costume Collage		•			•	•	•		•
Section IV: Ceramics									
IV-1 Clay Candlesticks	•	•			•		•	•	•
IV-2 Ceramic Coil Mirrors	•	•			•		•		•
IV-3 Clay Face Necklaces		•			•	•			•
IV-4 Heart Frames and Necklaces	•	•		•	•		•		•
IV-5 Clay Bells		•		•	•		•		•
IV-6 Clay Pockets		•			•		•		•
IV-7 Coil Pottery	•	•			•		•	•	•
IV-8 Clay Appliqué Plaques	•	•		•	•		•		•
IV-9 Evergreen Plaques	•	•	•		•		•		•

Focus Areas

	line	shape	value	color	texture	perspective & proportion	pattern & composition	cultural enrichment	creative thinking
Section V: Paper Crafts									
V-1 Torn Paper Trees	●	●		●	●	●	●		●
V-2 Paper Bag Houses		●		●	●	●			●
V-3 Stitched Paper Puppets	●	●		●		●		●	●
V-4 Quilling Valentines	●	●			●	●	●	●	●
V-5 Paper Sculpture Animals		●		●	●	●			●
V-6 Witches	●	●		●	●	●			●
V-7 Oaktag Houses	●	●				●		●	●
V-8 Tissue Paper Fish Kites		●		●		●		●	●
V-9 Two-Cardboard Relief	●	●	●	●	●		●		●
V-10 Dancing Bears	●	●		●		●			●
V-11 Landscape in the Round	●	●		●	●	●			●
V-12 Lunar Shadow Boxes	●	●	●	●		●			●
V-13 Paper Bag People		●		●	●				●
V-14 Tissue Paper Silhouettes	●	●	●			●		●	●
Section VI: Printmaking									
VI-1 Handprints	●	●			●				●
VI-2 Texture Prints	●	●	●	●	●		●	●	●
VI-3 Chalk Prints		●	●	●			●		●
VI-4 Two-Color Styrofoam Prints	●	●	●	●	●		●		●
VI-5 Tempera Tile Prints	●	●	●	●	●		●		●
VI-6 Leaf Prints	●	●	●	●	●		●		●
VI-7 Gadget Prints	●	●	●	●	●		●		●
Section VII: Weaving									
VII-1 Straight Weaving	●			●	●		●	●	●
VII-2 Circle Weaving	●	●	●	●	●		●	●	●
VII-3 Paper Weaving	●	●	●	●	●		●	●	●
VII-4 Ojos de Dios	●		●	●	●		●	●	●
VII-5 Straw Weaving	●	●	●	●	●		●	●	●
Section VIII: Crafts									
VIII-1 Stuffed Butterflies		●		●		●	●		●
VIII-2 Planetary Architecture	●	●		●	●	●			●
VIII-3 Point-to-Point Yarn Designs	●	●		●			●		●
VIII-4 Soft Foam Masks	●	●		●	●	●		●	●
VIII-5 Constructional Problem Solving	●	●	●				●		●
VIII-6 Complete the Picture		●	●			●			●
VIII-7 Wood Sculpture	●	●		●	●	●	●		●
VIII-8 Hand Puppets		●		●	●	●		●	●
VIII-9 Aluminum Plaster Casting	●		●		●			●	●
VIII-10 Metal Masks	●	●		●		●			●

INTERMEDIATE LEVEL

Focus Areas

	line	shape	value	color	texture	perspective & proportion	pattern & composition	cultural enrichment	creative thinking
Section I: Drawing									
I-1 Action Figures	●	●				●			●
I-2 Pen and Ink Owls	●	●	●	●		●	●	●	●
I-3 Two-Pencil Drawings	●	●	●				●		●
I-4 Musical Still Life	●	●		●		●	●		●
I-5 Personality Profiles	●	●	●			●	●		●
I-6 Window Views	●	●	●	●		●	●	●	●
I-7 Half-Face Portraits	●	●	●		●	●		●	●
I-8 Whale Dreams	●	●				●			●
I-9 Architecture in Our Town	●	●			●	●			●
I-10 Portraiture	●	●	●	●	●	●		●	●
I-11 Two-Point Perspective	●	●				●		●	●
I-12 Bicycle Drawings	●	●				●	●		●
I-13 Texture Drawings	●	●	●		●	●	●		●
I-14 Idiomatic Illustrations	●	●		●					●
Section II: Painting									
II-1 Foil Clowns	●	●		●	●		●		●
II-2 Window Portraits	●	●		●	●	●			●
II-3 Jungle Resist	●	●	●	●	●	●	●		●
II-4 Pointillism		●	●	●			●	●	●
II-5 Sand Paintings		●		●	●			●	●
II-6 Warm and Cool Colors		●	●	●		●		●	●
II-7 Monochromatic Painting		●	●	●		●		●	●
II-8 Multimedia Slides	●	●	●	●	●		●		●
Section III: Color and Design									
III-1 Art Object Designs	●	●	●	●			●		●
III-2 Magazine Textures	●	●	●		●	●	●		●
III-3 Paper Mosaic		●	●	●	●		●	●	●
III-4 Geometric Pictures	●	●	●	●			●		●
III-5 Rainbow Pictures	●	●		●			●		●
III-6 Multimedia Mosaic	●	●	●	●	●		●		●
III-7 Negative/Positive Designs	●	●	●				●		●
III-8 Design a Van	●	●		●		●			●
III-9 Candy Jars	●	●		●	●			●	●
III-10 One Line Only	●	●	●		●		●		●
III-11 Color and Design	●	●	●	●			●		●
III-12 Radial Designs	●	●	●	●			●		●
III-13 Optical Illusions	●	●	●				●		●
III-14 Lettering	●	●					●		●

Focus Areas

	line	shape	value	color	texture	perspective & proportion	pattern & composition	cultural enrichment	creative thinking
Section IV: Ceramics									
IV-1 Clay Mobiles		•		•	•		•		•
IV-2 Treasure Boxes	•	•		•	•		•		•
IV-3 Clay Dinosaurs		•		•	•	•		•	•
IV-4 Clay Houses	•	•		•	•				•
IV-5 Clay Animals	•	•		•	•	•			•
IV-6 Dream Car	•	•		•	•	•			•
IV-7 Clay People	•	•		•	•	•			•
Section V: Paper Crafts									
V-1 Setting the Stage for Halloween	•	•		•	•				•
V-2 Halloween Mobiles	•	•		•			•	•	•
V-3 Three-Dimensional Silhouettes	•	•	•			•			•
V-4 Cut Paper Masterpiece	•	•	•	•		•	•		•
V-5 Paper Towers	•	•	•	•			•		•
V-6 Kites	•	•		•			•		•
V-7 Colonial Pull Toys	•	•		•		•	•	•	•
V-8 Flying Tetrahedrons	•	•					•	•	•
Section VI: Printmaking									
VI-1 Styrofoam Texture Prints	•	•	•	•	•		•	•	•
VI-2 Linoleum Block Prints	•	•	•	•	•		•	•	•
VI-3 Silk-Screen Prints	•	•	•	•			•		•
VI-4 Glue Prints	•	•	•	•	•		•		•
Section VII: Weaving									
VII-1 Op-Art Weaving	•	•	•				•		•
VII-2 People Weavings	•		•	•	•		•	•	•
VII-3 Textural Weaving	•	•	•	•	•		•	•	•
VII-4 Basket Weaving	•	•			•		•	•	•
Section VIII: Crafts									
VIII-1 Puppet on a String		•		•	•	•		•	•
VIII-2 Papier-mâché Flu Bugs		•		•	•	•		•	•
VIII-3 Fluorocarbon Foam Sculpture	•		•	•	•	•		•	•
VIII-4 Creative Problem Solving	•		•	•	•		•		•
VIII-5 Gnomes	•			•	•	•			•
VIII-6 Milk Jug Masks	•			•	•	•			•
VIII-7 Butterfly Batik	•	•	•	•			•	•	•
VIII-8 Copper Foil Jewelry	•	•					•	•	•
VIII-9 Robots	•	•		•	•	•			•
VIII-10 Balsa Wood Houses	•	•		•			•		•
VIII-11 Marionettes	•	•		•	•	•		•	•
VIII-12 Sand Casting	•	•			•		•	•	•
VIII-13 Clone Soft Sculpture		•		•	•	•			•
VIII-14 Creativity Kits	•	•	•	•			•	•	•
VIII-15 Animation	•	•	•	•				•	•
VIII-16 Zodiac Banners	•	•	•	•	•	•	•		•

ART CURRICULUM ACTIVITIES KITS
Intermediate Level

Level 4

In *Action Figures*, further emphasis on body proportion and movement of the body are brought into play using basic geometric ovals and circles. The art medium of pen and ink is introduced in *Pen and Ink Owls,* while different parts are textured, shaded, stippled, cross-hatched, and otherwise experimented with, using pen and ink techniques. In *Two-Pencil Drawings,* the student holds two pencils in one hand and creates a random design. Together with the technique of shading, this lesson demonstrates three-dimensional representation in drawing. The concept of still life is introduced in *Musical Still Life* and the composition of objects, reinforcing the use of overlapping, is studied as is further work on proportion. *Personality Profiles* explores the concept of the silhouetted profile and of drawing objects based on aspects of each individual's personality.

Pen and Ink Owls

Level 5

Window Views emphasizes distance, depth, foreground, middle, and background pictorial elements as well as the concepts that objects appear smaller as they recede in space and that dark colors show distance and light colors show closeness. Facial features and proportions are studied in *Half-Face Portraits* and in *Whale Dreams,* fantasy is given further exploration. Advanced observation of architectural techniques and a beginning awareness of perspective play a primary role in *Architecture in Our Town.*

Architecture in Our Town

Level 6

Portraiture studies the proportion of facial features and their placement in a portrait. Further study in perspective on a more formal scale is conducted in *Two-Point Perspective.* In *Bicycle Drawings* detail and proportion, as well as close observation, come into play. *Texture Drawings* reinforces the use of textural elements as an integral part of designing and adding interest. *Idiomatic Illustrations* looks at some commonly used expressions in a new light.

Two-Point Perspective

Action Figures

ACTION FIGURES

Materials:

- pencil and eraser
- drawing paper
- markers and crayons

Directions:

1. One way to make drawing people a little easier is to think of the body as a series of simple shapes joined together.

2. To begin, ask someone to be your model. Ask this person to "freeze" in action, perhaps pretending to be swinging a bat or running or stretching. Any "action" pose will do.

3. Since it is very difficult for the model to hold such a pose for long, you will have to work quickly.

4. Begin by sketching a stick figure with your pencil. Show the direction of the head, a bend in an arm, the tilt of the hips, and so forth. This sketch should be *very* simple, and your model should relax as soon as you've finished it. See example A.

5. The next step is to "fill out" your stick figure. See example B.

6. The last step (example C) is to outline your new form carefully and add clothes. Afterward, you can erase your inside guidelines and "color in" your person.

7. A field trip to a gym class would be a helpful activity to include with this project.

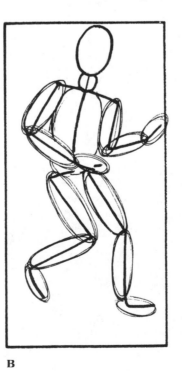

A   B   C

Pen and Ink Owls

PEN AND INK OWLS

Materials:

- newspaper
- drawing ink and steel nibbed pens
  or
- a variety of thin felt markers
- 9″ × 12″ white drawing paper

Directions:

1. Begin by spreading newspaper under your drawing paper. This is very important because some drawing inks are permanent and can stain your working surface. Needless to say, you should be careful when working with inks not to spill them or let them spatter or drip.

2. After setting up, sketch your owl on white drawing paper. Try to make it large. Fill in as much detail as possible with your pencil.

3. Now dip your pen in the drawing ink and wipe it against the inside of the bottle as you remove it, so that it won't drip. On a piece of scrap paper, experiment with some of the different line types you can use to make an interesting drawing. See the following examples.

   See if you can invent some new styles.

4. Now begin to fill in the owl. Try to use the widest variety of strokes possible. You may wish to add an interesting background.

Two-Pencil Drawings

TWO-PENCIL DRAWINGS

Materials:

- newsprint or practice paper
- 1 sheet of white construction paper, 12″ × 18″
- 2 pencils and an eraser
- crayons and markers

Directions:

1. These drawings are fun to make but will take a little practice on a piece of newsprint paper.

2. Start by holding two pencils in your right or left hand (whichever you normally draw with) as shown in the illustration. Keep your hand very stiff and upright. While you are getting the feel for it, try "dragging" your pencils across the paper in different directions. It is important that you apply equal pressure to both pencils as you draw.

3. After some practice you can begin to try curves, loops, and circles.

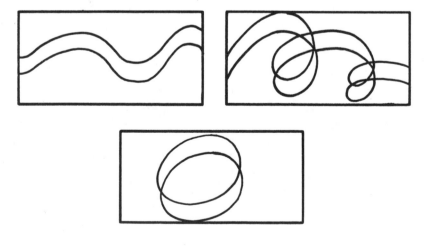

You may even want to write your name.

4. By now I'm sure you've noticed how your pencils create a double image. In order to use this to its best advantage in creating a design, you may need to fill in the double image as if it were a solid ribbon with black on one side and white on the other.

Before

After

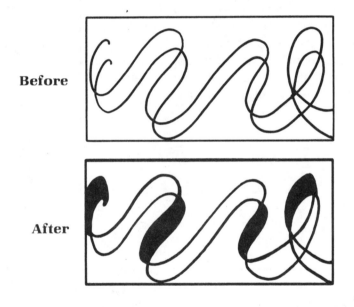

5. Use your new skill to create a picture or design.

6. If you can't quite get the hang of using both pencils in one hand, you can achieve the same result by taping the two pencils together and drawing with them as if they were one.

Musical Still Life

MUSICAL STILL LIFE

Materials:

- manila paper
- musical instruments
- white drawing paper, 12″ × 18″
- pencil and eraser
- thin, black, permanent market
- watercolors and brushes

A **still life** is a picture representing objects, such as fruits and flowers, which are neither moving nor alive. Still-life studies have been used by artists as a subject for hundreds of years because they can be composed of items an artist can find right in his or her home. Also, many techniques of art, such as shading, overlapping, proportion, and composition, can all be practiced using a still life. Representing different surfaces, such as glass, metal, and wood, are easily practiced in a still life using different lines, textures, and shading.

Directions:

1. Very often things that we imagine will be difficult to draw become simplified after observing them closely.

2. Start by creating a very detailed drawing of an instrument—any instrument. Make it large enough to fill your sheet of manila paper. When it is completed, set it aside.

3. Set up a still life or an arrangement of musical instruments in such a way that you can see them from your drawing position. Any type of instrument will do, from harmonicas to saxophones. Students who take music lessons often bring their instruments to school and may be able to provide you with your models.

4. Spend some time just looking at the composition of instruments and at the arrangement of the shapes they present.

5. Next, begin to sketch what you see. You may wish to show only one or two instruments from the arrangement and draw them in great detail. Or, you may want to sketch the overall composition of all of the instruments with less emphasis on individual detail.

6. When your drawing is completed, outline it with a thin, permanent, black marker and paint it carefully with watercolors.

Personality Profiles

PERSONALITY PROFILES

Materials:

- 1 sheet black construction paper, 12″ × 18″
- 1 sheet white construction paper, 12″ × 18″
- scissors
- white glue
- pencils, markers

Directions

1. To begin, you will need to cut out a silhouette of your profile. Find a strong light in your work area and place it in such a way that it casts a shadow of your profile on the wall.

2. Tape the white construction paper to the wall in the spot where your shadow appeared. Now ask a friend to trace the shadow of your profile onto the paper.

3. Afterward, remove the white paper from the wall and place the black paper beneath it. Then, following your outline, cut through both sheets of paper.

4. This will give you two identical profiles. Use the white one to show things about yourself—things you like to do, places you like to go, things that you think about, dreams that you may have. These will show people not just how you look but also who you are.

5. When you are finished coloring in your drawings, place this white profile on top of the black one, allowing the black one to protrude a bit in order to emphasize your profile.

Window Views

WINDOW VIEWS

Materials:

- tempera paint and brushes
- markers
- pencils and erasers
- rules
- one sheet of 12″ × 18″ manila

Directions:

1. The object of this type of picture is to use as many pictorial devices as possible in order to create the illusion of depth. To begin, choose a window—any type of window—such as a store window, a windshield, a porthole, or even the cracked window of a haunted house.

2. Outline your basic window shape and include as many details as possible, such as modeling, glass panes, shutters, curtains, latches, and so forth.

3. Next, begin to draw the scene visible from your window. This might include hills and valleys, oceans and ships, stars and planets, or the contents of a shop.

4. Whatever you draw, remember to make things smaller and smaller as they get farther and farther away from your window. Some things will overlap; this helps us see what things are in front of other things.

5. Now you are ready to show things that are in front of your window: a person looking out the window, a cat on the window sill, a hanging plant, a chair or other furniture, wallpaper, paints on the wall, and so forth. Remember that the more detail you add, the more convincing your picture will be.

6. Finally, paint your pictures using cool colors (blues, greens, grays, purples) to make some parts recede and warm colors (orange, yellow, red, brown) to make other parts come forward.

Half-Face Portraits

HALF-FACE PORTRAITS

Materials:

- ruler
- magazines
- pencil and eraser
- 9″ × 12″ drawing paper
- scissors
- glue

Directions:

1. Look through a magazine for a large, full-face photo. Carefully cut it out of the magazine.

2. Next, use a ruler to draw a line down the middle of the face; then cut along this line.

3. Trim any outer edges or advertising from the photo; then glue it on one side of your paper.

4. Now fill in the missing half of the face, matching the features by studying the photo. Use your pencil to create shadows and highlights. This will make the face appear to be three-dimensional.

Whale Dreams

WHALE DREAMS

Materials:

- pencil and eraser
- 12″ × 18″ white paper
- thin, black marker

Directions:

1. Think of the dreams you have had—perhaps doing something you couldn't or wouldn't do in real life.
2. Draw what you think a whale might dream.
3. You may include several scenes, overlapping in different sections of your paper.
4. Try to think of a fantasy to include in the dream that a whale might have, such as flying, being a ship for people to ride on, and so forth.
5. Try to include a nightmare portion. Think of what a whale might fear.
6. Trace over all the lines with the marker and color in certain parts for emphasis.
7. Try to include a drawing of the whale.
8. If there are any empty spaces between portions, draw in various repeated patterns, such as stars, stripes, spirals, and zigzags, and fill these in or outline them in marker.

Architecture in Our Town

ARCHITECTURE IN OUR TOWN

Materials:

- 12″ × 18″ white drawing paper
- pencil and eraser
- photos of architecturally interesting houses in your town

Architecture is the art of building, and it includes the design, construction, and decorative treatment which give a building a certain character or style. American architecture has gone through many stylistic periods, including the English style of Jamestown and of Plymouth, the formal periods of the Georgian, the Federal, and the Greek Revival eras, the simplicity of the New England saltbox, the log cabin of the westward expansion, the Victorian Era, and modern design beginning with the architect Frank Lloyd Wright.

The Georgian style was balanced and often featured fanlighted doorways. Such doorways were sometimes pillared, pedimented and graced with a Palladian window above and a hip roof.

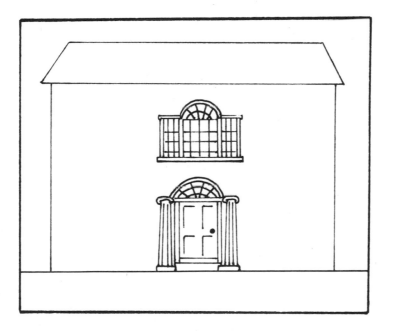

The Federal Period added more ornamentation and a "monitor roof" to light the stairwell. The windows were often larger, sometimes reaching to the floor.

The Greek Revival house often had a portico with columns.

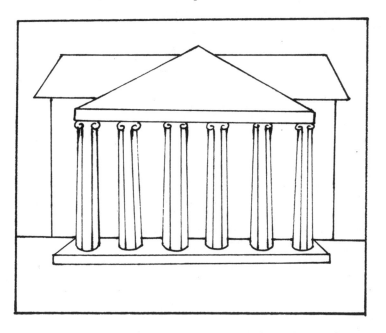

The Victorian house often had wooden "gingerbread" work, cast-iron tracery, patterned shingling, intricate brickwork, and other more lavish decoration than before.

See if you can locate some of these parts in the house you have chosen and identify its period.

Directions:

1. Remember, in drawing architecture, all vertical lines remain vertical; it is only the horizontal lines that slant.

2. Keep in mind that as an object gets farther away from you, it appears smaller.

3. Study the photo you chose and notice these principles.

4. Draw the photo, including all of the details and using the principles mentioned above.

5. Shade in certain areas to give emphasis and contrast to your drawing.

6. Include bushes, walks, and part of the lawn to provide a "base" for the house.

Portraiture

PORTRAITURE

Materials:

- pencil and eraser
- paper

Portraiture is the art of creating a likeness of a person. Pictures that an artist paints of himself are called self-portraits. Rembrandt van Rijn, one of the world's most famous artists, was a great portraitist. During his lifetime, he created many penetrating portraits of different people and more than 100 self-portraits. These self-portraits show him at various ages and in different moods, and they all help to tell us the story of his life.

Directions:

1. Begin by drawing a large oval.
2. Measure the length of your oval and draw a horizontal line at the halfway point.
3. Now measure the length of this line and divide the length into five equal sections.

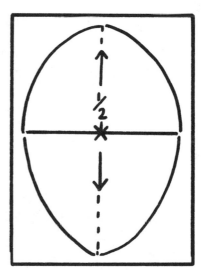

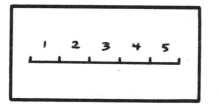

4. Divide the same length in half and draw a line extending from the forehead to the chin.

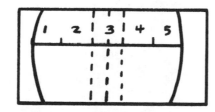

5. Extend the lines to the right and left of your center line from the forehead to the chin.
6. Now measure the distance from your horizontal line to the chin and find the halfway point. Draw a horizontal line at this point.
7. Next, measure the distance from this line to the chin and draw another horizontal line at the halfway point.
8. Now that all of your guidelines are complete, use them to determine the correct placement of your subject's features.
9. After you have drawn all of the features, you can erase your guidelines and use your pencil to do shading and modeling.

Two-Point Perspective

TWO-POINT PERSPECTIVE

Materials:

- 12″ × 18″ paper
- pencil and eraser

Perspective is the art of showing on a flat surface various objects, architecture, or landscape in such a way as to simulate (that is, give the illusion of) dimension and space between objects near and far away.

Directions:

1. Draw a line from side to side on your paper slightly below the middle as shown.

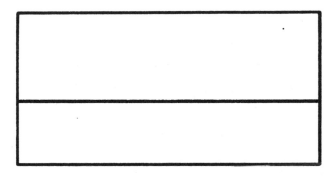

2. This is called the horizon line and represents where the sky meets the ground.
3. Place two *X*s on this line near the sides as shown:

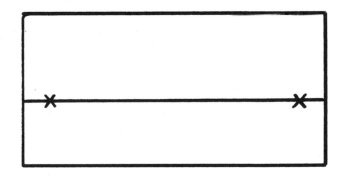

4. These are called the vanishing points.
5. Draw a vertical line between the *X*s as shown on the next page and connect the *X*s to the ends of the line.

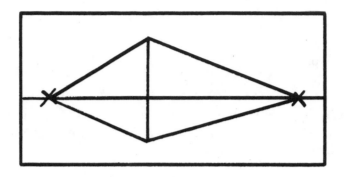

6. Now you can draw a building using your lines as shown in the illustration. The windows follow the same angles or lines.

7. These angles to the building and windows are optical illusions. You know that a building doesn't really slant like this, but it does look like this *because* objects appear smaller as they go back in space. A train track is a good example. It looks like art "A," not like art "B."

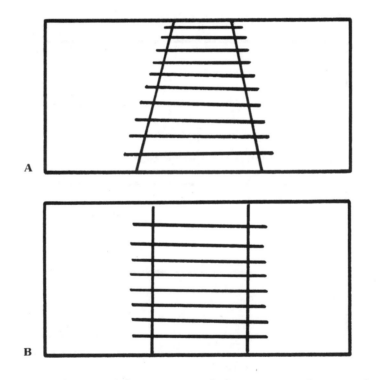

8. Now you are going to pick a corner of the room to draw. Pick an interesting corner with lots of objects and some furniture. A corner of a kitchen is a good choice.

9. If you draw it as shown in the following illustration, remember that the invisible dotted lines going back to the vanishing points still exist. Do not draw these in.

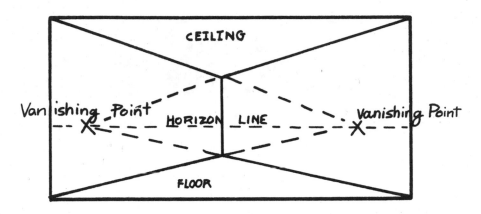

10. All the angles of tables, chairs, and pictures on the wall follow the angles of the floor and ceiling.

11. Remember all vertical lines will remain completely vertical; it is only the horizontal lines that angle or slant.

Bicycle Drawings

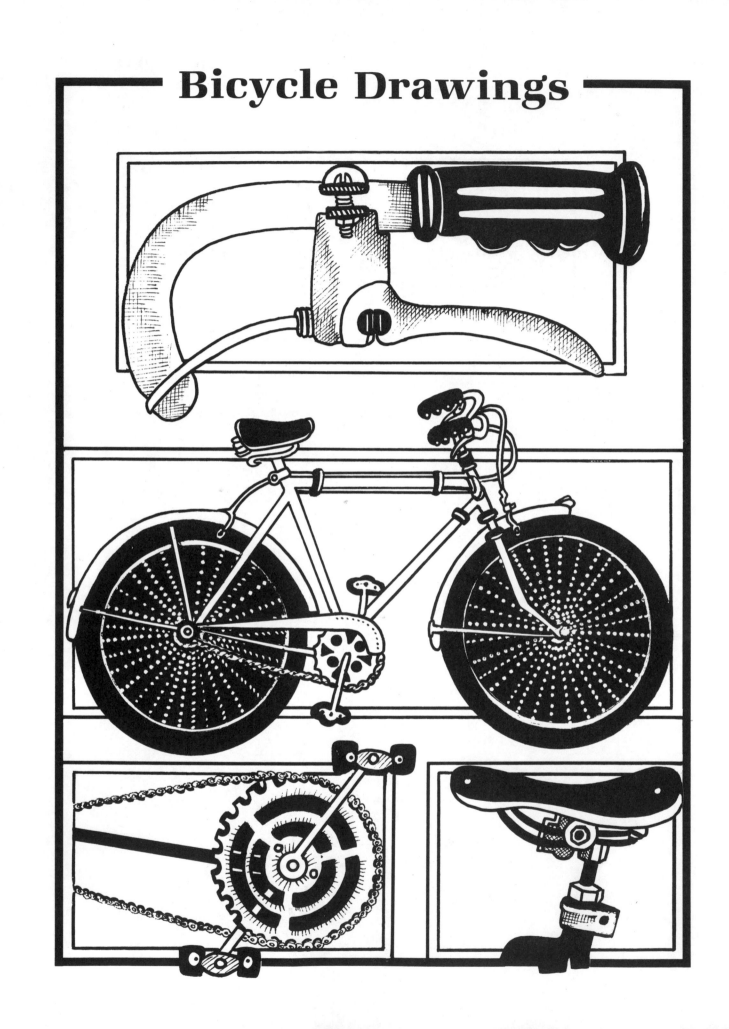

BICYCLE DRAWINGS

Materials:

- one two-wheeled bicycle
- 12″ × 18″ white paper
- pencil and eraser
- thin, black marker
- magnifying glass (optional)

Directions:

1. Set up a two-wheeled bicycle on a table so that you are viewing it directly from its side and can see both wheels.
2. Lightly draw two large circles on your paper where you think the wheels would be.
3. Remember to draw large enough so that the bike will fill the space of the paper.

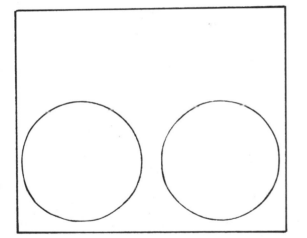 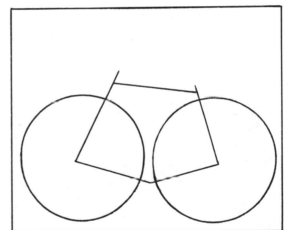

4. Study the angles of the main frame or bars of the bike and draw these lines in lightly.
5. Carefully observe the position of the handlebars, and draw them exactly as they appear. If one side of the handlebar obscures your view of the other side, simply draw the side you see.
6. Begin to sketch in the more detailed sections of the bike, the seat, the chain, pedals, fenders, and so forth.
7. Trace over all the pencil lines with a marker.
8. Erase any visible pencil lines.
9. As a follow-up exercise, try focusing on and magnifying one part of the bicycle and turning it into an exciting nonobjective drawing.

Texture Drawings

TEXTURE DRAWINGS

Materials:

- pencil and eraser
- 9″ × 12″ white drawing paper
- black, fine-point markers

Directions:

1. Examine natural objects—such as tree bark, corn husks, rocks, and insects' wings—for their textural qualities. Notice how textural patterns can be used to emphasize and contrast forms and space.

2. Study photos or slides of insects. Notice the body parts and the segments of the legs.

3. Draw an insect very lightly with a pencil and make your drawing large enough so that some parts extend off the paper. Essential details of the insect should be put into your drawing.

4. Outline your drawing with black, fine-point markers.

5. Divide the negative space (the space around the "positive" space) within the insect with light pencil lines to provide background shapes.

6. This breakup of the negative space gives the picture interest and variety.

7. With the markers, make patterns within these spaces.

8. This will develop many interesting designs, which will be striking in black and white and which will emphasize the difference between positive and negative space.

Idiomatic Illustrations

IDIOMATIC ILLUSTRATIONS

Materials:

- white drawing paper, 18″ × 24″
- pencil and eraser
- thin, black marker
- crayons

Idiomatic expressions are unique phrases that say one thing but mean something else. Confused? Take a look at the picture that accompanies this activity. This picture illustrates a commonly used idiomatic phrase. Can you guess what that phrase is? The picture shows us what the phrase *says*, but it does not show us what the phrase *means*. Do you know what the phrase means?

Directions:

1. See how many other idiomatic phrases you can add to this list.
   a. Your eyes are bigger than your stomach.
   b. You're the apple of my eye.
   c. Cat got your tongue?
   d. I'm so hungry I could eat a horse.
   e. Catch a tiger by the tail.
2. Select one or two phrases and see if you can illustrate them. Use a pencil to complete your drawing, and then outline your pencil drawing with a thin, black marker. Color with crayon if you wish.
3. When you're finished, see if someone can guess your idiomatic phrase just by looking at the picture.

Level 4

Foil Clowns presents the technique of painting on aluminum foil and reemphasizes the use of pattern and repetition. In *Window Portraits,* the use of protraiture and the proportion of features is further explored. The technique of "crayon resist" is examined in *Jungle Resist,* which affords the opportunity to create intricate designs and further expands on the use of fluorescent colors.

Jungle Resist

Level 5

Pointillism introduces the nineteenth century impressionist concept and the use of a tool other than a brush with which to produce a stippling technique. Also emphasized is how colors placed close together blend at a distance. *Sand Paintings* explores a different medium for painting. In *Warm and Cool Colors,* the "temperature" of a painting is explored.

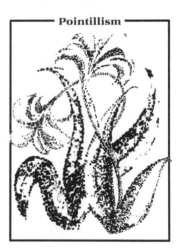

Pointillism

Level 6

Use of shades and tints of one color is presented in *Monochromatic Painting* as well as continued compositional exercise. In *Multimedia Slides,* various solutions and found objects are used with all the elements of design in art to construct a small scale composition which can be projected onto a screen.

Monochromatic Painting

Foil Clowns

FOIL CLOWNS

Materials:

- aluminum foil
- tempera paint and brushes
- one sheet of 12″ × 18″ manila paper
- masking tape
- liquid dish detergent
- pictures of clowns
  (from magazines, books, etc.)

Directions:

1. Begin by looking at pictures of clowns. Notice how many geometric shapes can be found in their faces, hats, and costumes.

2. Tear off one sheet of foil a little larger than your manila paper.

3. Next, fold the excess foil back over the edges of the manila paper and tape it to keep it in place.

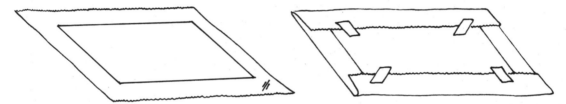

4. Start by drawing a large circle in the middle of your foil. Use the "wrong" end of the paintbrush to make your outline.

5. Next, place a large triangle on top of your circle and an oval around the bottom of it.

6. Next, see how many times a circle can be used to create features on your clown, such as eyes, nose, cheeks, and an open mouth, or polka dots and a pom-pom for the hat.

7. Add ears and hair and use a continuous line to create a collar inside your oval shape.

8. When all your outlining is done, begin to go over your outline with paint. A few drops of detergent should be added to the

paint in order to make it adhere to the foil. Fluorescent paint can look particularly good because it is so bright.

9. Painting outlines rather than "filling-in" will make the best use of your foil background. Also, by painting patterns or designs within these outlined shapes, you can create a shimmering quality in your work.

Window Portraits

WINDOW PORTRAITS

Materials:

- newspaper, sponges, water, brushes
- black tempera paint
- 2 drops of liquid dish detergent
- student models
- paper towels

Directions:

1. Student models are led outside and are then asked to stand in front of windows where they can be viewed by the students in the classroom.

2. Next, cover the floor or counter space directly in front of each window with newspaper and equip each artist with a paper cup of black tempera, a thin brush, and a sponge. Liquid detergent should be stirred into the tempera for two reasons: (1) to help the paint adhere to the surface of the window, and (2) to simplify the cleanup of any paints that may spill. Please note that too much liquid detergent may make the paint crackle and blister after it dries, so add detergent sparingly.

3. Now, begin by asking your models to freeze in one position. (Having them stare at a fixed point will help them to remain still.) Start outlining your model with black paint; follow the lines of the face, hair, and clothing. You can pretend you are tracing a photograph; this may help you to find your "outlines."

4. If you make a mistake, it is very simple to correct it by wiping it away carefully with a slightly damp sponge. Then, dry the area with a paper towel and start again.

5. When you are done outlining, remember to thank your model. You can "paint in" your person when your black outlines are dry, but you do not need a model for this step.

6. At different times of the year, you may wish to add or subtract clothing (hat, gloves, coats, and so forth) according to the weather.

Jungle Resist

JUNGLE RESIST

Materials:

- newspaper
- crayons (all but purple, brown, and black)
- 12″ × 18″ heavy, white paper

- pencil and eraser
- watered down black tempera and paint brush

Directions:

1. Study the jungle paintings of Rousseau.
2. Draw your idea for a jungle on manila paper. Include exotic, large-leaved plants, animals, and birds that are in trees as well as on the ground. Include textures in your leaves and in the skin coverings of the animals and birds.

3. Trace over your pencil outlines with crayon, press hard on the crayon as you do this.
4. Begin to fill-in outlined areas with various patterns and designs. Remember to use bright or fluorescent colors as these will show up best when your picture is painted.

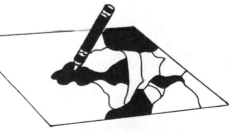

5. Place your picture on top of newspaper and paint across the entire surface with watered down black tempera.
6. The paint will "resist" your crayon lines and fill-in any empty spaces in your picture.

43

Pointillism

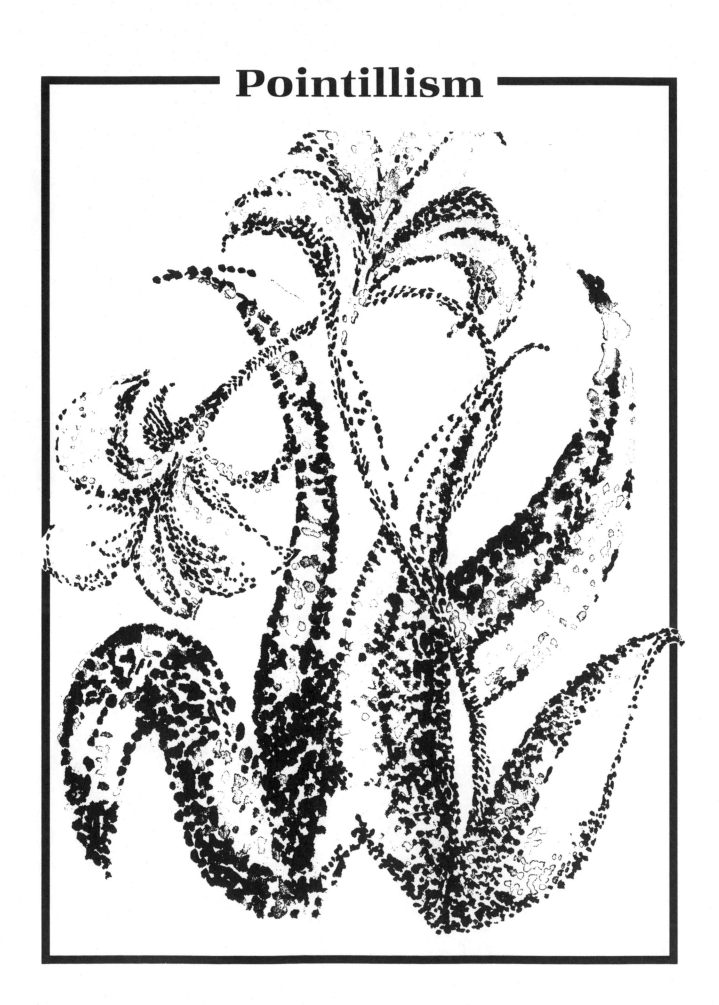

POINTILLISM

Materials:

- 9" × 12" drawing paper
- pencil and eraser
- oil pastels or Cray-Pas®
- slides or reproductions of paintings by Georges Seurat

Directions:

1. Pointillism was a style of painting popularized by a small group of French painters at the turn of the century. The most famous Pointillist painter was Georges Seurat, and it would be very helpful to look at examples of his work before starting this lesson.

2. When you look closely at a Pointillist painting, you will notice the use of tiny dots instead of areas of solid color. By using dots of color the artist can create many interesting effects.

3. One effect you can experiment with is color mixing. Place tiny yellow dots right next to tiny blue dots, and then step back from your picture. Do you see a new color?

4. Next, place tiny red dots next to tiny blue dots and step back. What do you see? If yellow and blue dots appear to look green when you step back and blue and red dots appear to look purple, you are on the right track. If you do not see any change perhaps it is because you made more blue dots than yellow ones or more red dots than blue. Keep experimenting to see what other combinations you can create.

5. After experimenting, choose a subject for your painting and lightly sketch it onto your white paper.

6. Then, starting with your lightest colors, begin to fill in your picture with tiny dots of color. You can do this by tapping your paper with the Cray-Pas®. Many dots close together will make a color look darker. This is good to know for creating shadows and outlines.

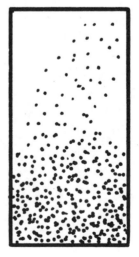

Sand Paintings

SAND PAINTINGS

Materials:

- one sheet of black paper, 12″ × 18″
- pencil
- watered-down, white glue
- glue brush
- paper cup full of sand
- newspaper

The Navajo Indians of America were probably the most famous at using **sand painting** as part of several important healing ceremonies. Their sand was ground from nearby cliffs, shells, charcoal, and pollen. Showing great skill, the artist reconstructed the designs from memory, dropping the colored sand with his thumb and forefinger. The designs showed many symbols for gods and spirits, the rainbow, mountains, animals, and plants. The Navajos, without a written language, kept their beliefs and legends alive with their sand painting.

Directions:

1. Sketch your picture on the black paper. Try to keep your picture simple and large.
2. Spread newspaper under your black paper. Begin to paint over your outlines with the glue mixture. Only paint a small portion at a time (so that the glue will not dry before you can add the sand).
3. Next, sprinkle sand over the portion of the picture you have painted. Let it set for a minute, and then lift your paper and pour the excess sand back into the paper cup.
4. Sand paintings look best when you use lines and designs rather than solidly painted areas to fill your picture.

Warm and Cool Colors

WARM AND COOL COLORS

Materials:

- 1 sheet of white paper, 12″ × 18″
- pencil, eraser
- ruler, tempera paints and brushes

Certain colors are thought of as warm and others as cool. We say this because certain colors, such as red, yellow, and orange seem to make us feel warm, while other colors, like blue and green, seem to make us feel cool. Most of the time, artists use a combination of **warm and cool colors** in their paintings, but sometimes to create a powerful effect they may decide to create a painting using only warm colors or only cool colors.

Directions:

1. In this activity, you will be able to observe this "effect" firsthand. You will be creating either a warm picture or a cool one.
2. Begin by drawing a picture on the white paper. If you are going to use warm colors, then draw a warm picture—for example, of a hot summer day, a race car, or of a forest fire blazing.
3. If you are going to use cool colors, then draw a cool picture—for example, an underwater scene, a snowball fight, or perhaps Eskimos ice fishing.

Monochromatic Painting

MONOCHROMATIC PAINTING

Materials:

- 12″ × 18″ manila paper
- white heavy paper, 12″ × 18″
- pencil and eraser
- 4 baby food jars
- popsicle sticks
- tempera paint
- masking tape

Monochromatic means a color scheme using shades and tints of only one color.

Directions:

1. Draw a sketch of a landscape for your painting. It could be underwater, in outer-space, or anywhere that you want it to be.
2. Copy it onto your white paper. An easy way to copy is to tape your first drawing under the white paper, tape this to a window, and trace the drawing.
3. A monochromatic painting uses dark and light shades or values of only one color.
4. Begin preparing your paints by filling two baby food jars each about one-third of the way with the one basic color you have chosen. To one jar, add nothing; to the other jar add a small amount of black paint.
5. Begin your third-color jar by filling it about one-third of the way with white paint. To this jar add a very small amount of your chosen color.
6. Make your fourth-color jar by filling it about one-third of the way with black paint. To this jar, add a small amount of your chosen color.
7. Mix each color with a popsicle stick. You should now have four very different shades or values of the color you have chosen.
8. You can now see that adding white always lightens a color and that adding black always darkens a color.
9. Using the correct size brush for each area, begin to paint in the landscape.
10. Try to use high contrast colors (colors that are light next to colors that are dark) to make the objects and shapes stand out clearly.
11. If you run into the problem of an object or shape not showing up, you can outline that shape with a darker or lighter color.
12. Remember never to paint next to a "wet" area. Paint in another part of the paper and come back to that area when it is dry.
13. When working this small, it is best to hold your hand as far down the brush next to the bristles as you can because you will have better control.

Multimedia Slides

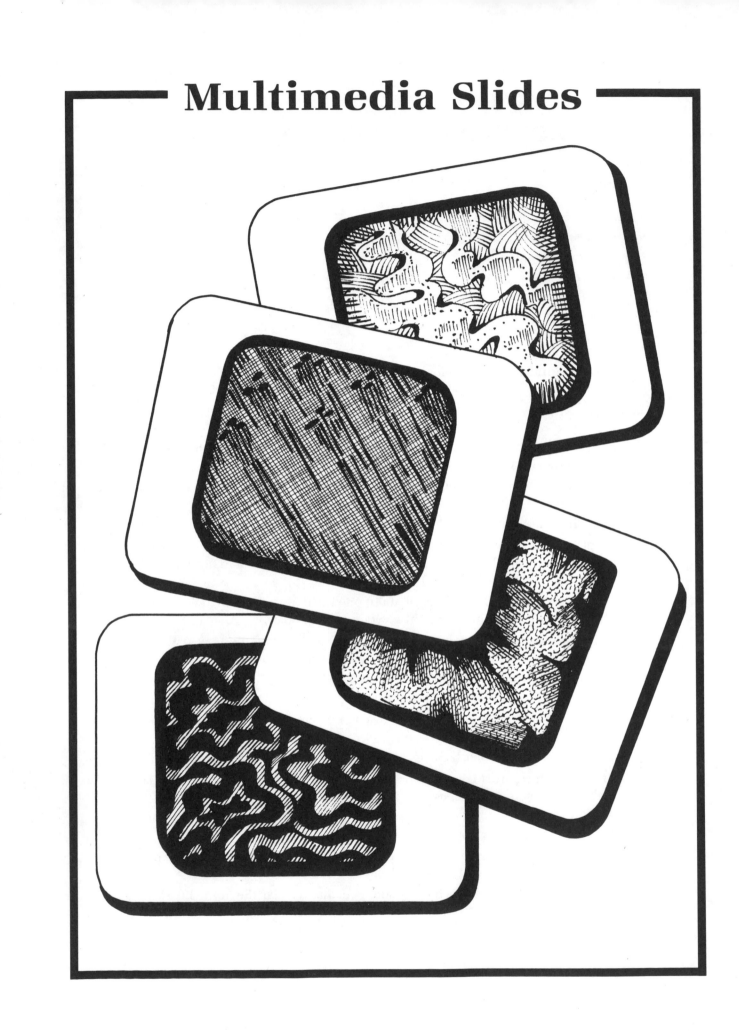

MULTIMEDIA SLIDES

Materials:

- slide projector
- 2″ × 2″ cardboard or plastic slide mounts
- treated plastic acetate cut into 4″ × 6″ squares
- 2″ acetate squares to cover and protect slides
- paper cups and popsicle sticks for mixing
- iron
- various solutions such as spray paints, hair spray, bleach, dyes, inks, and so forth
- eye droppers
- tissue paper, onion skins, hair, open-weave material, leaves, insect wings, and so forth

Directions:

1. Use the materials on the 4″ × 6″ acetate squares and develop slides by mixing and dropping solutions into liquids already on the acetate. Let dry.
2. Prepare a slide for each below:
   a. shape
   b. line
   c. color
   d. texture
   e. space
   f. light (transparent, translucent, opaque)
3. Examine the results, then select and cut out the most interesting 2″ square you can find in each of the larger pieces.
4. You may place additional "sheer" materials mentioned above on the acetate and then place a second piece of clear acetate on the painted surface of the slide to be mounted.
5. When ready to mount, make sure it fits into the inner frame of the slide mount. Then, fold the top of the slide mount over the two pieces of acetate and press the *sides* of the mount with a hot iron. This will cause the waxed edges of the mount to seal.
6. At another time, try gathering other materials brought in from home.
7. Images can be projected onto canvas for paintings.

Color and Design

Level 4

Art Object Designs takes a commonplace object and uses it as a design element and to reinforce the techniques of collage and overlapping. Visual, rather than tactile, texture is given concentration in *Magazine Textures* as is the study of the composition of the whole from parts. The technique of "mosaic" is introduced in *Paper Mosaic* and in *Geometric Pictures*. In these lessons, paper cut in geometric shapes is used to form a composition. The project *Rainbow Pictures* reinforces the use of paper and includes the use of the contrast of patterned paper with solid colors.

Paper Mosaic

Level 5

Advanced use of assorted materials is used in *Multimedia Mosaic*, which offers additional work in this art technique. Negative and positive areas are introduced in *Negative/Positive Designs* and are shown as an integral part of all artwork. Surface design is further studied in *Design a Van* as is further compositional exploration within a specified shape. *Candy Jars* provides continual compositional exploration including overlapping and objects placed on top of one another. In *One Line Only* creative problem solving using only one type of line alternating the length and width is explored.

Design a Van

Level 6

Color and Design involves a paper and color design project emphasizing shape and the use of repetition, and it is also an informal introduction to positive and negative design. *Radial Designs* emphasizes and reinforces pattern and repetition and introduces the radiating technique of creating a design. The concept of illusion in art design is explored in *Optical Illusions*, where precise graphic art is presented. *Lettering* introduces the art of calligraphy.

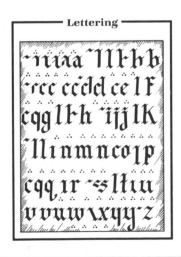

Lettering

Art Object Designs

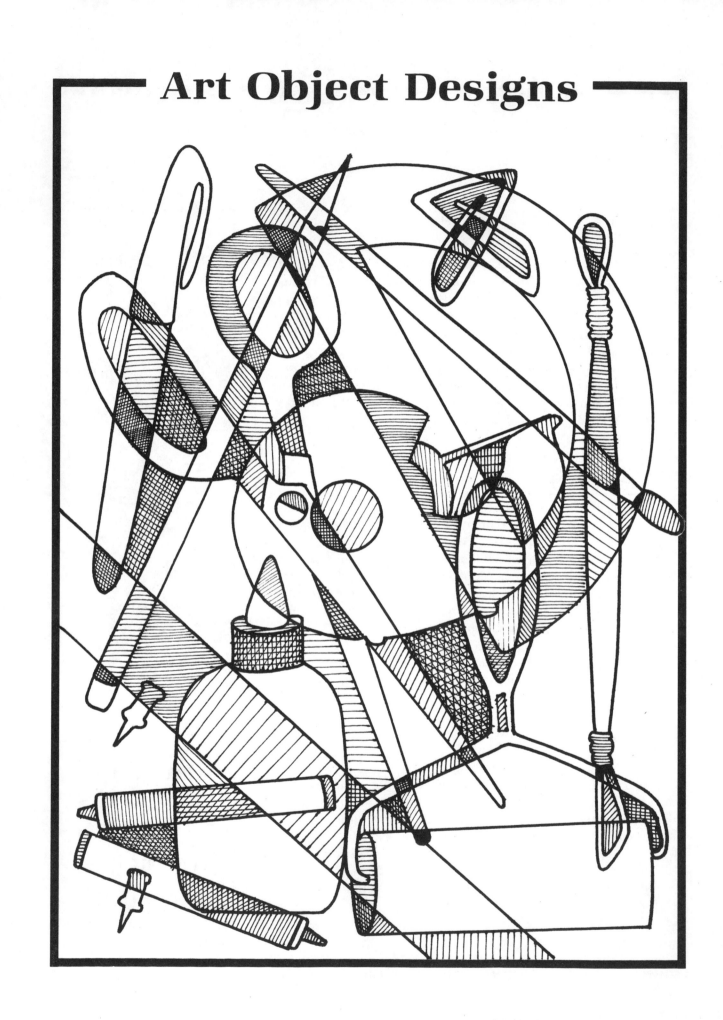

ART OBJECT DESIGNS

Materials:

- 1 sheet of white paper, 12″ × 18″
- pencils and kneaded eraser
- art equipment: rulers, tape, protractors, scissors, compass, paper clips
- thick, black marker
- colored markers or tempera paints and brushes

Directions:

1. Soften your kneaded eraser in the warmth of your hand and then remove a small piece of it and use it to secure an art object to your paper. This object might be any of the things that are listed above. With your object anchored in place, take a pencil and trace around it.

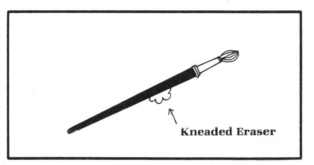

Kneaded Eraser

2. Continue to trace other objects, overlapping the objects but still doing complete outlines.

3. When your composition is complete, use your black marker to go over your pencil outlines. Remember to do complete outlines even when objects overlap.

4. After your black outlines are finished, you can begin to color in with markers (or tempera paints) the new shapes created by your overlapping outlines.

5. At this point, the objects themselves become less important and your new design emerges.

Magazine Textures

MAGAZINE TEXTURES

Materials:

- 9″ × 12″ oaktag
- magazines
- scissors and glue
- pencil and eraser

Texture is the surface of anything, from rough to smooth. It may be a real surface or a visual impression of a texture, such as an actual mountain range or a picture of one in a magazine.

Directions:

1. Cut out textural sections of magazine ads or illustrations until you have a good selection of colors and types.

2. Draw a simple landscape on the oaktag.

3. Cut sections with appropriate colors and textures to fit each object and glue them in.
4. Try to use light colors next to dark colors for contrast.

Paper Mosaic

PAPER MOSAIC

Materials:

- gummed paper tapes in a variety of colors
- 12″ × 18″ black paper
- pencil and eraser
- 12″ × 18″ manila paper
- egg carton
- glue
- scissors
- variety of metallic papers, colored magazines ads
- slides or photos of mosaics (see below)

A mosaic is a picture or decoration made by joining together minute pieces of glass, stone, tile, wood, or other substances of different colors.

Directions:

1. Study slides or photos of Greek, Roman, or Far Eastern mosaics.
2. Draw a single idea for your mosaic on the manila paper.
3. Next, place your manila paper drawing on top of the black paper, and then use a pencil to retrace all the lines in your picture. Press very hard on the pencil while doing this so that a clear impression of your picture will be made on the black paper.
4. Now, decide which colors of paper tape you will need for your picture, and then cut them up into tiny pieces. You may wish to use an egg carton to separate and save your multicolored pieces of paper tape.
5. Next, begin to fill in the various parts of your picture with the tiny pieces of colored tape. Place the shapes close together but not touching, as shown in the following example.

6. Try to place light colors next to dark colors for high contrast. This will make the objects show up more.
7. For interest, you might also want to use metallic paper or portions of the colored ads from magazines.

Geometric Pictures

GEOMETRIC PICTURES

Materials:

- 1 sheet of white paper, 12″ × 18″
- scissors
- white glue
- assorted colors of construction paper

Directions:

1. Begin by cutting up a variety of colored paper into an assortment of geometric shapes of all sizes, such as fat and skinny triangles, long and short rectangles, big and small circles, and so forth.

2. Now, begin to arrange these in different ways on your white paper. What can you combine your shapes to create? You may wish to overlap some shapes and also cut some new shapes to fit a particular idea.

3. Plan your finished picture and very lightly make pencil outlines to help you place your shapes in the right place. See if you can make a very detailed picture. You can create designs and patterns by repeating the same shape over and over again or by alternating a few different shapes repeatedly.

Rainbow Pictures

RAINBOW PICTURES

Materials:

- white glue
- multicolor strips of varying widths
- 2 sheets of black construction paper
- pencil and scissors

"**Collage**" is a French word that means gluing or pasting. As an art term it means to assemble, arrange, and paste materials to create an artistic composition.

Directions:

1. Using white glue, cover one sheet of black paper with a series of brightly colored paper strips of varying widths.

2. When dry, turn this sheet over and outline the things you wish to cut out to create your picture.

3. Next, place your cutouts on black construction paper and combine the lines and patterns to create interesting effects.

Multimedia Mosaic

MULTIMEDIA MOSAIC

Materials:

- seeds, beans, macaroni
- glue
- heavy cardboard, 12″ × 18″
- 12″ × 18″ manila paper
- pencil and eraser
- carbon paper

Directions:

1. Draw a simple idea for your mosaic.
2. Use carbon paper to transfer it to cardboard.

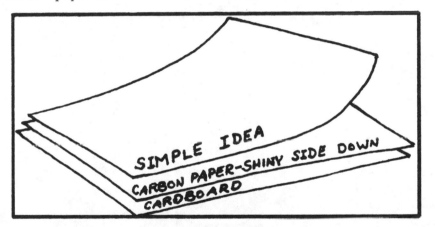

3. Divide your picture into areas and begin to glue different mosaic pieces into each. Be careful to place light-colored pieces next to dark-colored pieces to enable various objects to show up by this contrast.

4. All areas of the cardboard should be covered, so place the pieces close together.

Negative/Positive Design

NEGATIVE/POSITIVE DESIGNS

Materials:

- 9″ × 12″ white drawing paper
- white glue
- 4″ × 6″ black construction paper
- pencil
- scissors

Directions:

1. Center your 4″ × 6″ sheet of black paper on top of your 9″ × 12″ sheet of white paper and lightly trace around your black sheet. This outline will help you line up with your shapes later on.

2. Now, begin to draw and cut out shapes around all four sides of your black sheet. Place the shapes to the right of your pencil lines and keep them in order as you cut them out.

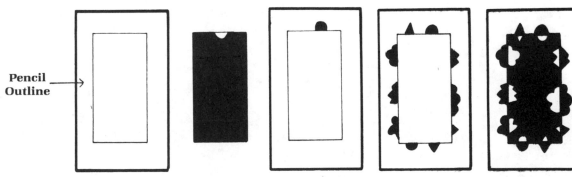

3. When all your shapes are cut out, glue down the large sheet first and then glue the shapes in their correct "reversed" place.

Design a Van

DESIGN A VAN

Materials:

- 12″ × 18″ paper
- pencil and eraser
- colored markers
- thin, black marker

Directions:

1. Draw the side of a van on 12″ × 18″ paper.

2. Draw a scene or design you would like to paint on the side of your van.
3. Outline all pencil lines with a thin, black marker and fill in the areas with colored markers.

Candy Jars

CANDY JARS

Materials:

- 12″ × 18″ paper
- pencil and eraser
- thin markers

Directions:

1. Draw a large glass jar with a lid big enough so that you fill the entire paper vertically.

2. Inside the jar, draw in as many different types of candy as you can remember.

3. Draw each candy in detail and make all of the candy appear piled on top of each other by overlapping the pieces and showing them at different angles.

4. Use the markers to color in the jar and candy.

One Line Only

ONE LINE ONLY

Materials:

- pencil and eraser
- 1 sheet of white paper, 9″ × 12″
- assorted thick markers and thin markers

Directions:

1. This is a lesson in creative problem solving. Your goal is to create a picture using only one type of line—a straight one.
2. Begin by lightly sketching your idea in pencil on the white paper.
3. Next, begin to fill in your picture with lines. You will have to alternate the length, the width, and the direction of your lines in order to make your drawing visible.

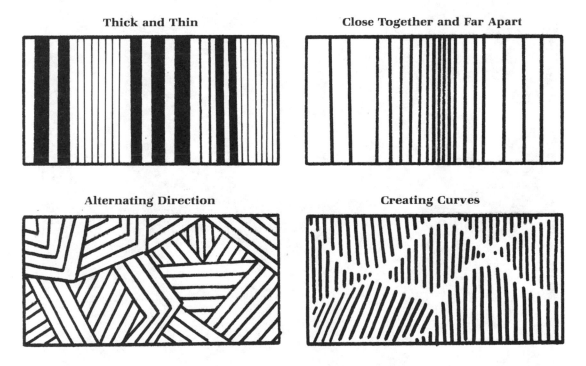

| **Thick and Thin** | **Close Together and Far Apart** |
| **Alternating Direction** | **Creating Curves** |

Color and Design

COLOR AND DESIGN

Materials:

- 18″ × 24″ construction paper
- pencils and erasers
- sharp scissors
- paste or glue
- sixteen 4½″ × 6″ rectangles of construction paper (4 each of 4 different colors)

Directions:

1. In order to create 16 rectangles, fold a sheet of 18″ × 24″ construction paper in half four times.

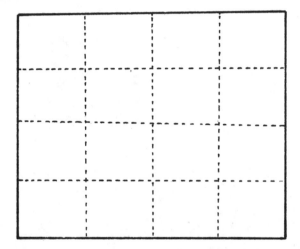

2. Next, choose four colors and cut out 16 rectangles 4½″ × 6″ in size (four in each color).

3. Choose a shape for each color category. Shapes that touch the tops and sides of the rectangle seem to work best. See the following illustration.

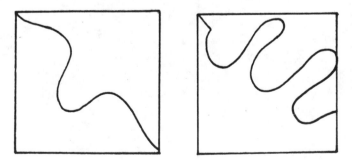

4. Cut out three identical shapes in each category using your first shapes as patterns.

5. Place four different shapes in each row and continue to do this in each subsequent row.

77

Radial Designs

RADIAL DESIGNS

Materials:

- pencils
- crayons
- watered-down, black tempera paint
- rulers
- manila or white paper

Directions:

1. What do a dart board, a starfish, a ferris wheel, and a flower have in common? For one thing, they are all good examples of radial designs. Radial designs are generated outward from a center point creating a circular pattern or design.

2. Find the center of your paper and mark it with a pencil dot.

3. Next, use your ruler to draw (*very lightly*) one line from your dot to the center top of the paper and another line to the center bottom. Then, make a line that goes from your center dot to the edge of each side of your paper. Next, draw a line from the top left side of your paper to the bottom right and another one from the top right to the bottom left side of your paper. These lines will serve as guidelines as you build up your design.

4. Starting at your center dot, begin to create shapes that will radiate toward the edges of your paper. For example, suppose you choose a triangle as your first shape. To make it radiate from the center, you would also make an identical triangle opposite your first one and then a triangle on each side. Notice that your design has changed to a square when it is complete.

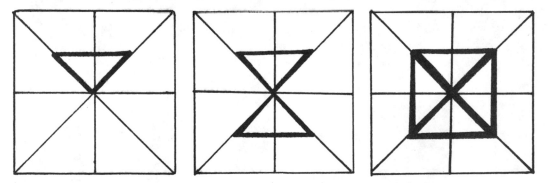

5. Continue to build up your design one shape at a time. You will be surprised at how many times it changes.

6. When you are done with your design, go over it in crayon. Press very hard and try to avoid using dark colors. You can make new patterns with color now by filling in some shapes with dots and others with stripes or wavy lines.

7. When you are done, brush the tempera over your design, painting evenly in rows and being careful not to repaint any areas.

Optical Illusions

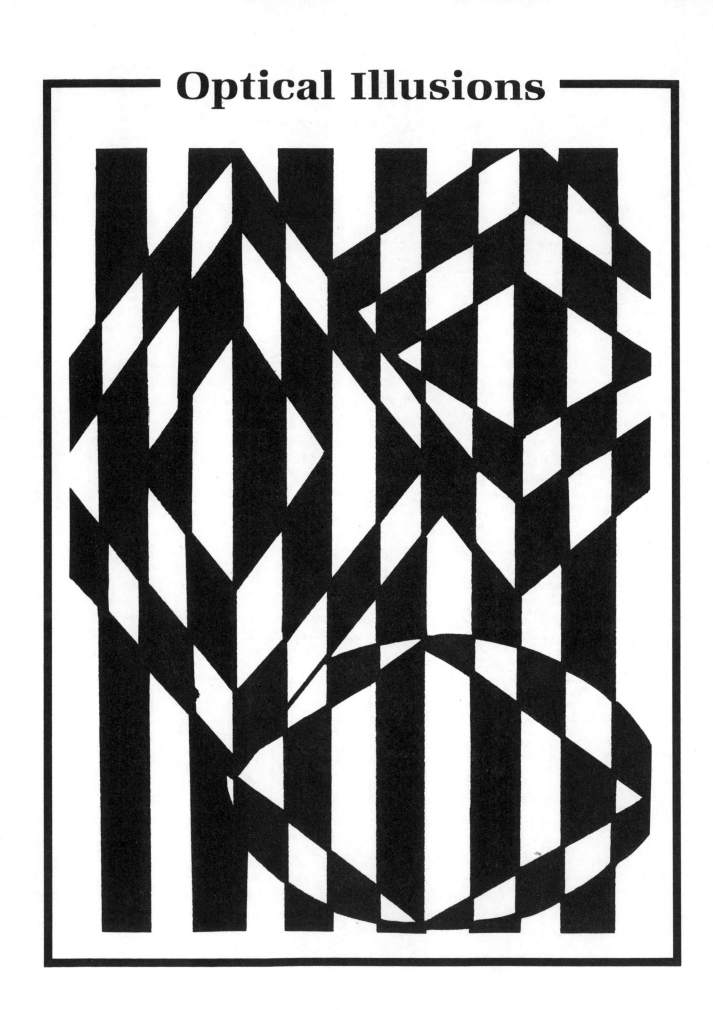

OPTICAL ILLUSIONS

Materials:

- pencil and eraser
- 9″ × 12″ white paper
- thin, black markers
- medium, black markers
- ruler and compass

Directions:

1. Measure your paper into ½″ sections and draw vertical lines across the paper as shown:

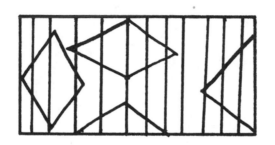

2. Inside, draw one large geometric shape. Next, repeat the shape inside or next to the first in varying sizes until the space seems filled as shown.

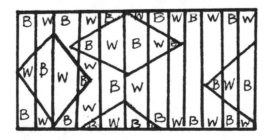

3. Begin with the top of the vertical space on your left and moving down, label lightly with a pencil each space you meet, alternately beginning with *B* for black and then *W* for white as shown. Continue until all spaces are marked by a *B* or a *W*. Alternate the labeling with each row or space.

4. When all spaces are labeled, begin to carefully color them in using the black markers in the areas labeled *B*.

5. When you are finished, erase all the *W*s.

Lettering

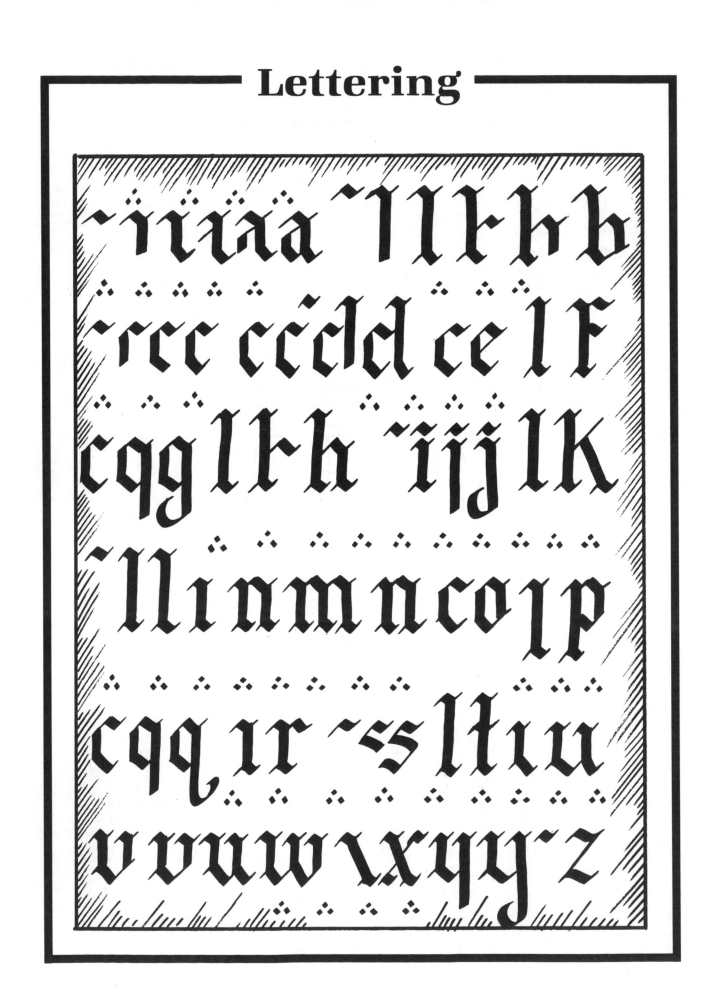

LETTERING

Materials:

- chisel point markers
- graph paper
- practice paper

Directions:

1. The letters you see in the illustration can all be created by using combinations of a few simple strokes.

2. First, familiarize yourself with the pen, noting that a chisel point or calligraphy marker has a tip shaped like this. This enables it to make thick as well as thin lines. Try making both on a piece of practice paper.

3. Using graph paper, you are ready to learn your first stroke, which is a thick, vertical line. Try to make these very straight.

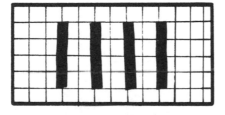

4. The next stroke consists of two thin, diagonal lines connected by one thick one.

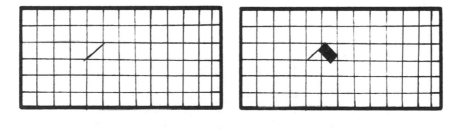

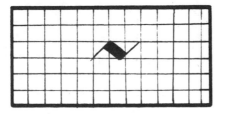

Practice these until they are easy to do. Try making some longer than others. See the following example.

5. By combining the two strokes already learned, you can create a shape repeated very often in this alphabet. This shape is a letter *C*.

Stroke 2
Stroke 1
Stroke 2

6. By looking at the alphabet in the illustration, see if you can find the *C* in the following letters.

7. When practicing your alphabet, always break the letter down into the strokes you recognize before starting. See the following examples.

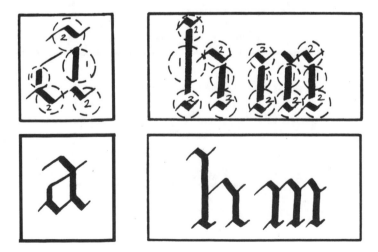

Level 4

The concept of a mobile in clay is introduced in *Clay Mobiles* and the slab technique is reinforced. In *Treasure Boxes*, appliqué is given further emphasis as is advanced work in using the slab to create a box.

Clay Mobiles

Level 5

The concept of hollowing out is advanced in animal construction in *Clay Dinosaurs*, while continued work with slab and architectural elements is explored in *Clay Houses*.

Clay Dinosaurs

Level 6

Advanced study in animal observation and construction is carried forth in *Clay Animals*. In *Dream Car*, a further exercise using the slab is explored as is incised surface design. *Clay People* presents the clay construction of a human form incorporating all the elements presented in drawing the figure.

Clay Animals

Clay Mobiles

CLAY MOBILES

Materials:

- clay
- rolling pin
- newspaper
- pencil
- cookie cutters (optional)
- manila paper
- nylon fishing twine or string

A **mobile** is a hanging or standing construction or sculpture made of delicately balanced, movable parts.

Directions:

1. On a piece of manila paper, plan your mobile and sketch it. Try to make your top piece and hanging pieces relate either through shape or idea. The example shows the daylight on top and the evening hanging in small pieces (the moon and stars).

2. When your sketch is complete, cut out your top piece and make a pattern of your smaller pieces. Place these on top of clay that you have rolled out to be about ¼″ thick.

3. Cut out your clay shapes by either outlining them with a pencil or tracing around your paper shape with a dull knife.

4. On your top piece, make one hole in the center of the top with a pencil. Then make five or six holes about ½″ from the bottom of your top piece. See the illustration.

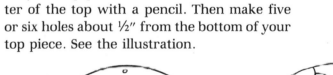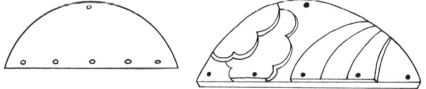

5. Next, decorate this piece by drawing shapes on it with a pencil or other clay tool, or build up the surface by adding clay shapes to it.

6. These can be put aside to be dried and later fired. When this process has been completed, they can be painted.

7. Cut out your small shapes with a paper pattern in the same way you cut out your top piece. You may also substitute cookie cutters if they will give you an appropriate shape. Make a small pencil hole in the top and bottom of each piece. The number of pieces you make will vary according to how full you want your mobile to look. Make a few extra shapes in case any break during the drying or firing process.

8. When all of your shapes have been fired and painted, use string or fishing twine to attach them to your top piece.

Treasure Boxes

TREASURE BOXES

Materials:

- cardboard
- ruler, pencil, eraser, and scissors
- clay or kiln firing or self-hardening clay
- two 10″ lattice strips
- rolling pin
- modeling tools
- mat
- glaze
- cloth
- slip (water mixed with clay to the consistency of heavy cream, which is used to join clay pieces together)
- paste brush

Directions:

1. Using the cardboard, measure and draw some rectangles or squares as templates for the bottom and sides of your box.
2. On the mat, roll out a ball of clay between two lattice strips to ensure a uniformly thick slab.

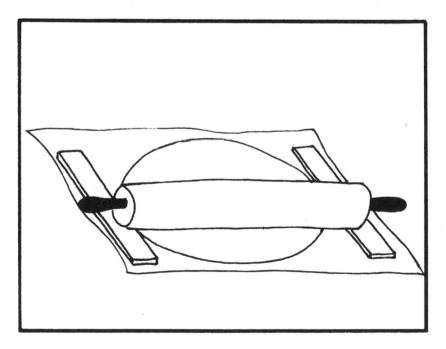

3. Lay the cardboard shapes on the slab and, using a thin modeling tool, cut around the cardboard and remove the excess clay.

4. Score the edges of the bottom of your box with a modeling tool and place some slip along the edge with a paste brush or with your finger.

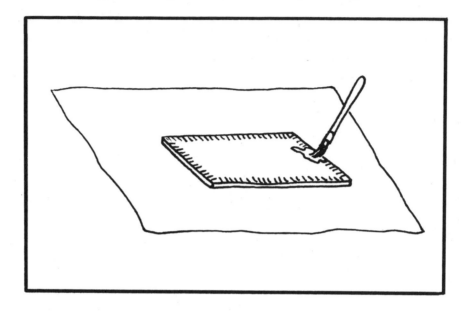

5. Set your first wall on one of these edges; score both ends of this side slab and add some slip.

6. Continue doing the same with the other sides of your box. Join the corners using scoring and slip and, in addition, weld the clay together using your fingers or a modeling tool.

7. Inside each corner, place vertically a very thin coil and weld or blend one into each side to provide strength.

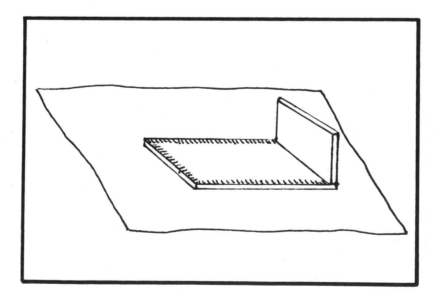

8. Coils may be added between the slabs to make a more interesting box, and they may also be used as a top edging or as a decoration on the box.

9. Try to make your box interesting enough to tempt someone to want to open it to discover its contents.

10. Measure the top for a lid and cut out a cardboard template.

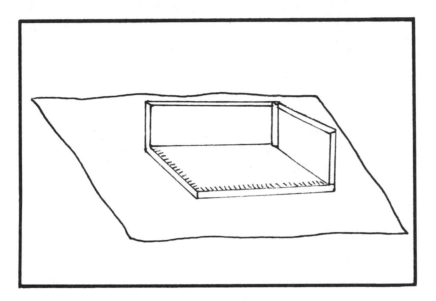

11. Roll out and cut a slab for the top and let this dry separately from the box.

12. Again, coils may be added to the top for interest.

13. Handles may be incorporated.

14. Let your box dry slowly with a damp cloth.

15. Fire and glaze.

Clay Dinosaurs

CLAY DINOSAURS

Materials:

- kiln clay or self-hardening clay
- modeling tools
- newspaper
- clay mats
- 12″ × 18″ paper
- pencil and eraser
- spoon

Directions:

1. After research, draw a contour drawing of the dinosaur you want to model.
2. Observe the shape of the body and start by modeling this.
3. Hollowing out forms is necessary when clay is to be fired in a kiln.
4. Hollow out the inside with a spoon or a wire-ended, loop modeling tool until the walls are about the thickness of your little finger.
5. Wad newspaper up tightly and stuff it inside the body of your dinosaur until it is completely filled.
6. Next, observe the legs. Are the shapes of the front legs the same as the back? Repeat the steps above for hollowing. Attach the legs by placing them where you want them and by adding more clay to make the joint strong. Finish by using your fingers to smooth out the surface of the joint.
7. Follow the steps above with the head, neck, and tail.
8. Use your tools to add any texture you desire to the skin.
9. Let dry slowly with a damp cloth draped over the form.
10. Fire and glaze.

Clay Houses

CLAY HOUSES

Materials:

- 9" × 12" paper
- photo of the front of your house
- pencil and eraser
- kiln-firing clay
- clay mat
- modeling tools
- wood slats, ¼" × 1'
- rolling pin

Direction:

1. Draw a simple contour of the front of your house using the photograph. Cut out the drawing of your house.
2. Roll out clay between the slats so that you have a slab as large as your cutout drawing.
3. Using a thin modeling tool, cut around your drawing like a giant cookie.
4. Using a pencil, add lines for windows, doors, and so forth as they appear in your photograph.
5. Roll out additional slabs and cut out some of these parts to add in a clay-appliqué technique, which will give your house a relief effect.
6. Using a tool in a twirling motion, make two holes at the top of your clay house about ½" from the edge so that you can hang your model.
7. Let it dry slowly under a damp cloth.
8. When leather-hard, brush off any excess bits of clay.
9. Let dry completely.
10. Fire and glaze.

Clay Animals

CLAY ANIMALS

Materials:

- clay
- modeling clay tool
- wire-looped clay tool
- clay mat
- newspaper
- pencil and eraser
- paper

Directions:

1. Draw a picture of the animal you wish to make. Pay attention to the details here so that you can use your drawing as a reference later while working on the clay.

2. Study your drawing and begin forming the body shape—usually an egg shape.

3. Add the legs next and decide whether you plan to make a reclining, sitting, or standing animal. Part of this will depend on whether the thickness of your animal's legs is sufficient to support the weight of its body when standing.

4. Clay parts must be added carefully and joined by smoothing the two parts together. You may even add a little additional clay when necessary for extra strength.

5. Scoop out the body with a wire-looped clay tool until no part of the body is thicker than your thumb.

6. If necessary, fill with crunched-up newspaper. This will support the body while you are working on it and will burn up in the kiln. Consequently, you do not have to remove the newspaper before you fire your clay model.

7. Next, add the neck and head, hollowing them out if they are thicker than your thumb and adding a hole in the body connecting with the hollow of the neck to let the air escape during firing as shown. If the legs are thicker than your thumb, they must also be hollowed out.

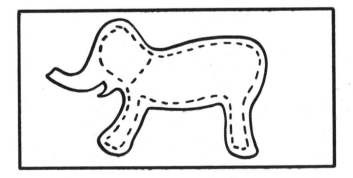

8. Add any details, smooth the clay so no cracks remain, and add skin textures or other features with modeling tools.

Dream Car

DREAM CAR

Materials:

- clay
- slip
- modeling tools
- mat
- rolling pin
- ¼″ × 1′ wooden slats
- 9″ × 12″ oaktag
- scissors
- ceramic glazes
- acrylic paint
- brushes

Relief is the projection of a part from the surface in sculpture or similar work.

Directions:

1. Draw a picture of your dream car on the oaktag.

2. Cut out the pattern, roll out a clay slab between the wooden slats, lay your pattern on the slab, and cut it out carefully. Remove the excess clay.

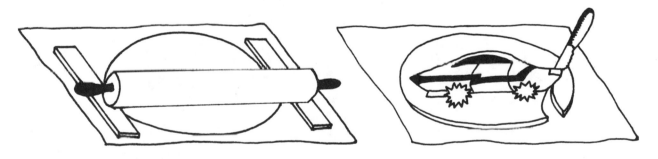

3. Using a pencil, draw in details from your drawing such as doors, headlights, windows, decorations, tires, and so forth.

4. Using other clay slabs, cut out some of these parts and attach them to your clay slab car using some slip and a modeling tool to join.

5. Let dry; fire; glaze or paint. If desired, fire again.

Clay People

CLAY PEOPLE

Materials:

- clay
- clay mat
- clay tools
- glaze or paint and acrylic polymer

Directions:

1. Start with a piece of clay a bit larger than a ¼-pound stick of butter.
2. The entire figure, with the exception of the arms, should be shaped from the single piece of clay.
3. "Slice" one end of the clay so that two segments can be shaped to form the legs and feet.
4. The other end should be pinched and molded to form the neck and head.
5. Roll out two coils of clay for the arms and then attach them to the torso.
6. Once the basic shape is formed and the proportions established, positioning of the figure should be determined.
7. Avoid stiff, rigid positions in favor of those which are more natural and relaxed.
8. Position yourself in a pose you want your clay person to take and study how the arms and legs arc bent. Get into the position yourself to get the idea.
9. Add details and finishing touches to give personality and expression to the figure.
10. Let dry, fire, and glaze, or paint and coat with acrylic polymer.

Level 4

The project *Setting the Stage for Halloween* involves more advanced paper sculpture techniques within a confined space to create a stage setting, while *Halloween Mobiles* introduces the concept of a "mobile." *Three-Dimensional Silhouettes* provides further use with the silhouette as an art technique and more experience with precise paper cutting.

Three-Dimensional Silhouettes

Level 5

Cut Paper Masterpiece presents the concept of reducing a picture to its basic geometric shapes. *Paper Towers* examines repetition and pattern in cut paper designs to create a three-dimensional art form. The project *Kites* involves designing within an unconventional surface shape—a diamond—and provides further work with basic kite construction. *Colonial Pull Toys* introduces an historical use of art in toy construction, increased practice with characterization and an understanding of body parts in action.

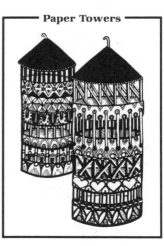

Paper Towers

Level 6

Flying Tetrahedrons explores a more advanced kite construction.

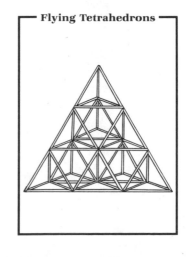

Flying Tetrahedrons

Setting the Stage for Halloween

SETTING THE STAGE FOR HALLOWEEN

Materials:

- cardboard box
- construction paper
- variety of papers (metallic, fluorescent, and so forth)
- scissors
- glue, masking tape, clear tape
- thin wire
- cotton
- pipe cleaners
- popsicle sticks
- markers

Directions:

1. Cut off the flaps on the box and cut down two corners as shown. The box should look like this.

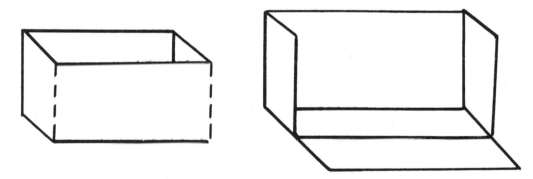

2. Glue paper on the inside and bottom of the box to simulate sky and ground.

3. If desired, glue paper to simulate hills in the background.

4. Imagine that you are designing a stage set for a play about Halloween. What would you want to include to create a scary atmosphere?

5. Review some basic paper sculpture techniques you might use:

Curling

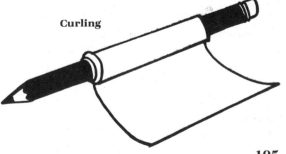

Fringing

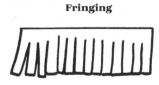

Tabs   Cones

6. Begin by constructing a castle or a haunted house, as shown. Make it have three sides by folding and give it tabs so that it will stand. Cut out doors and windows. Draw shapes to simulate stone, brick, wood, and so forth on the outside walls before standing.

Glue

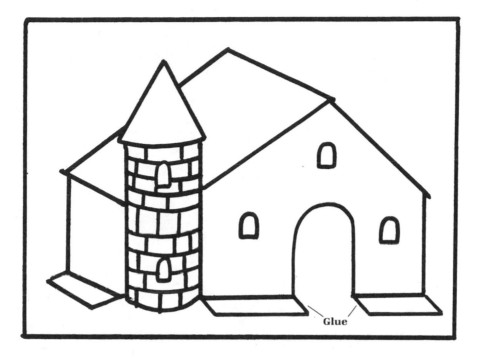

Glue

7. Glue the flaps and set up your construction.

8. Add other objects to create an eerie effect, such as ghosts, monsters, vampires, trees with scary objects in them, gravestones, and bridges over water filled with horrible creatures.

9. Use the thin wire to suspend flying witches, ghosts, bats, and so forth.

10. You may want to add a moon, dark clouds, or lightning to create the mood.

Halloween Mobiles

HALLOWEEN MOBILES

Materials:

- manila paper
- 12″ × 18″ orange posterboard
- 9″ × 12″ black posterboard
- nylon fishing twine
- hole puncher
- markers
- scissors
- glue

Directions:

1. To begin, you'll need to make a large pumpkin shape on your orange posterboard. The best way to do this is to stand up, hold your pencil the way you would hold a piece of chalk, and move your arm in a circular motion right *above* your paper. When your imaginary circle is large enough to take up the whole paper, begin to let your pencil lightly touch the surface of the paper. Do this many times until you have a dark outline. See the following example.

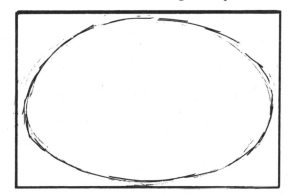

2. Cut along your outline and erase the extra lines. Next, sketch the lines which show the sections of the pumpkin's face. Afterward, go over these lines in black marker. Repeat this step on the other side also.

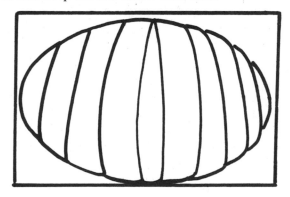

3. Next, sketch the line that will divide your pumpkin's face in half. It will also define your eyes, so draw it carefully. See the examples.

4. Afterward, cut along your lines; then draw a mouth and nose on both the front and back of your pumpkin and color them in with a black marker.

5. Next, make a pattern for your bat eyes by folding a piece of manila paper in half and drawing a shape as shown from the fold.

6. Place your pattern on the black posterboard and trace and cut out two bats. Also, draw and cut out a stem and glue it to the top of your pumpkin.

7. Next, use a hole puncher to make holes in the following places.

8. Connect all the pieces with fishing twine and hang.

Three-Dimensional Silhouettes

THREE-DIMENSIONAL SILHOUETTES

Materials:

- 1 sheet of white paper, 9″ × 12″
- 1 sheet of black paper, 9″ × 6″
- pencil and eraser
- ruler
- scissors
- white glue
- crayons and markers

Directions:

1. Holding your white paper horizontally, draw ½″ margins along the right and left sides of your paper. Fold the paper toward the center along your pencil lines. Then use crayon or markers to create a scenic background for your silhouette.

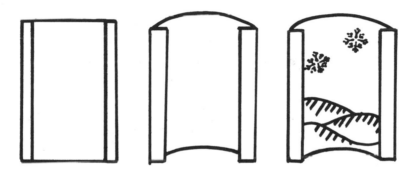

2. Next, holding your black paper vertically, draw ½″ margins along all four edges. Then, draw your silhouette making sure it is touching at least one of the four margins.

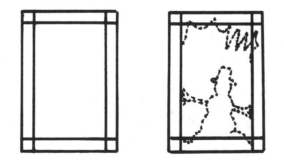

3. Now, cut away the areas surrounding your silhouettes. Then add glue to the left and right margins.

4. Attach the black paper to the white paper by lining up the glued margins with the folded white margins.

Cut Paper Masterpiece

CUT PAPER MASTERPIECE

Materials:

- reproduction of a famous painting
- tracing paper
- 1 sheet of black paper, 12″ × 18″
- various sheets of colored paper
- pencil and eraser
- thin, black marker
- scissors
- glue

The illustration for this activity is based on the painting *Woman Pouring Milk* by **Jan Vermeer.** Vermeer lived and painted during the seventeenth century in Holland. Most of his paintings show us simple scenes of Dutch life. Vermeer is known as the "painter of light" because of the skillful and sensitive way he was able to capture the effects of light on the surfaces it altered.

Directions:

1. You will be doing something very unusual in this lesson—something that you've always been told *not* to do. You will be tracing someone else's work. You will select a reproduction of a famous work and then place tracing paper on top of it and begin to outline the forms.

2. As you do this, shapes and forms you had hardly noticed will begin to emerge. Examine the different types of lines the artist has used. If you were drawing the picture, how would you have drawn the same thing?

3. The first illustration (Figure A) shows one small section of the large illustration in detail. It shows the right arm from the shoulder to the elbow. Compare this to Figure B, which shows the same area drawn simply. We can see that the artist has very carefully rendered every fold and crease in the fabric in Figure A after close observation and study. We notice that this attention to detail makes Figure A much more interesting to look at than Figure B.

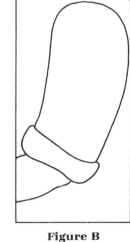

Figure A   **Figure B**

4. In Figure C, we see a tracing of just the head, which reveals all the small changes in light, shadow, and color. Your tracing does not have to be this detailed, but it does show you how complicated parts can be broken up.

5. After you have finished outlining, begin to cut out your tracing, one piece at a time. As you do this, place it on a sheet of construction paper which is the appropriate color. Then trace it and cut it out.

6. Glue this shape onto your black construction paper. Continue to assemble your masterpiece in this way, almost like a puzzle.

Figure C

Paper Towers

PAPER TOWERS

Materials:

- assorted sheets of construction paper
- white glue or paste
- markers
- stapler
- scissors
- pipe cleaner

Directions:

1. a) Fold one sheet of construction paper in half lengthwise.
   b) Then fold it in half lengthwise again.
   c) When you open it up, flatten it out and cut along your three fold lines. This will give you four strips of paper that are the same length and width.

2. Now take two strips and overlap and glue them together to create one very long strip. Do the same thing to the two remaining strips.

3. Next cut out multicolored geometric shapes and glue them in a decorative pattern on the long strips.

4. When this is done you are ready to attach thin paper strips to the bottom of your long strip. Try to space these evenly across a row.

5. When these are dry, you can attach your second long strip to the bottom with glue.

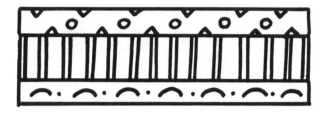

6. Continue to make row after row in the same manner. The more rows you make, the taller your tower will be. You can also experiment with strips of paper that connect the rows by using a criss-cross or diagonal pattern.

7. When all your rows are connected and dry, you can roll your tower into a cylinder shape by matching up the ends of the long strips and stapling them together.

8. To make a roof for your tower cut out a black circle (about the size of a dinner plate), and then cut away a slice of it. Next, pull one edge of the circle under the other and staple them together as they overlap.

9. Attach four wide strips to the base of this black top, and then staple the other ends of those four strips to the tower. Next, twist one end of a pipe cleaner into a knot and insert the other end through the point of the tower top. This will make it easy to hang your tower up so that it can spin in the breeze.

Kites

KITES

Materials:

- 12″ × 18″ manila paper
- pencil and eraser
- tempera and brushes
- heavy, butcher-grade paper
- scissors
- carpet twine or other strong, thin string
- rulers
- 2 sticks (one 30″ and one 36″) of narrow lattice notched in the ends
- glue

Kite making dates back to early Chinese history. Kites were used to deliver messages and even in warfare. Today, kites are used for enjoyment and range in size, shape, and materials.

Directions:

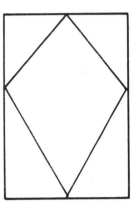

1. Draw a diamond shape for your kite on manila paper as shown.

2. Draw a design or picture inside this shape using all the space to compose your idea.

3. Lay the two sticks crossed with the shorter one horizontally across the longer one 7″ down from the top (marked at the middle of 15″). Glue them together at this point and wrap a narrow piece of masking tape around them to hold them until they are dry. Make sure the sticks are not crooked.

4. When the sticks are completely dry, run the string through one notched end and tie; pass it on to the next notched stick, keeping the string taut and then on to the next, and the next, and then back to the last stick and tie.

5. Lay the strung kite frame on heavy paper and trace the string kite shape, holding it firmly with your other hand while you trace.

6. Remove the frame and add a 1″ border all the way around to allow for some paper to be folded and glued over the string frame.

7. Draw your design or picture on the large paper kite form and paint. Let dry.

8. Lay your painted kite design under your frame, backside up, and carefully fold 1″ borders over the string and glue them down. Let dry.

9. Bridle the kite on the front side as shown. The two strings should be tied about 4″ away from the surface of the kite.

10. Attach flying string to the point where the two strings are joined.

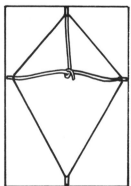

Colonial Pull Toys

COLONIAL PULL TOYS

Materials:

- manila paper
- pencils, eraser, markers
- posterboard in assorted colors
- 1 plastic straw
- scissors
- tape
- yarn or string
- 4 brass fasteners
- hole puncher

Directions:

1. Begin by sketching your character on manila paper. Keep your shapes simple. Arms and legs should be drawn straight.

2. Next, cut out your entire figure and then cut the arms and legs from the torso. Use these cutouts as patterns on the posterboard. Trace around them and cut them out.

3. Use the hole puncher to place holes as shown. Then overlap the holes and join the parts with brass fasteners.

4. Now use markers or crayons to color in and decorate your character.

5. Next, cut four 1″ lengths from the plastic straw. Attach one to the back of each arm and leg with tape as shown.

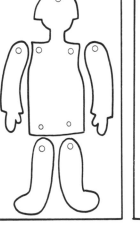
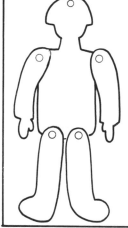

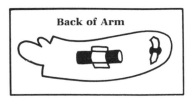

Back of Arm

6. Cut four 15″ lengths of string or yarn. Tie a large knot at the end of each one and thread one through each straw as shown.

7. Gather all four strings into a knot and trim the strings to the same length.

8. Pull the strings and watch what happens.

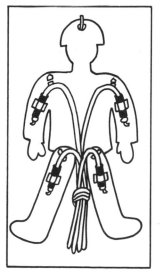

Flying Tetrahedrons

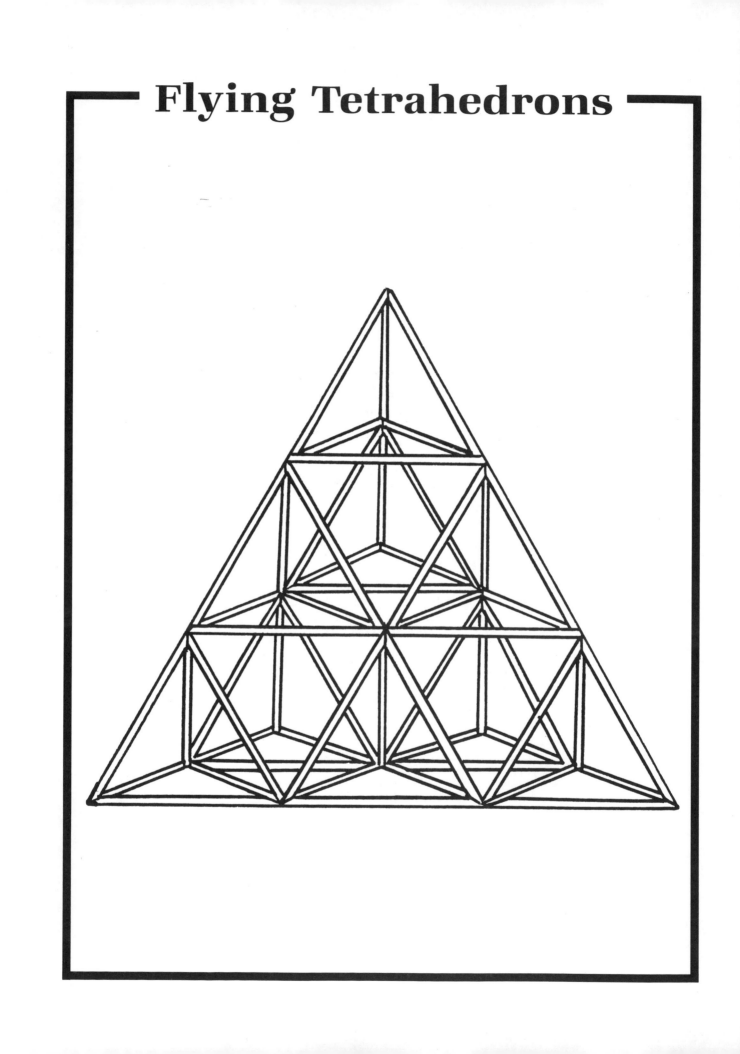

FLYING TETRAHEDRONS

Materials:

- white glue
- 60 paper straws
- brightly colored tissue paper
- scissors and string

A **tetrahedron** is a triangular pyramid.

Directions:

1. To begin making your kite, start by carefully joining six straws together with glue as shown. Then cover two sides with tissue paper. This completes one unit. In order to make a kite you need ten units.

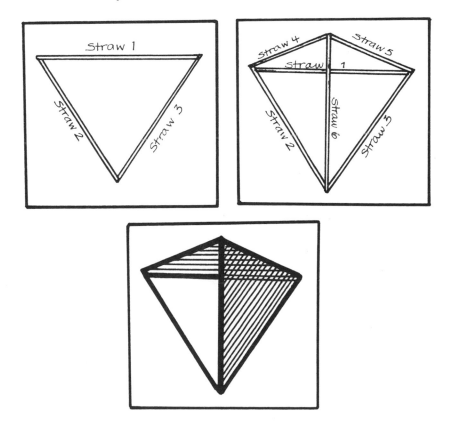

2. When you have completed ten units, assemble your kite with glue by aligning the corners of each unit and making sure they are all facing in the same direction.

3. Attach a string to each corner of your base and then join these three strings together in a knot. Add a long strip to this knot and go fly your kite.

Printmaking

Level 4

Styrofoam Texture Prints explores printmaking further by using incised shapes to create various textures.

Styrofoam Texture Prints

Level 5

Linoleum Block Prints introduces a new medium, linoleum, and reinforces the use of texture and pattern, as well as negative and positive areas in printmaking.

Linoleum Block Prints

Level 6

Silk-Screen Prints illustrates a more advanced printmaking technique using a stencil, while *Glue Prints* explores the "line" quality of printmaking in a relief style.

Silk-Screen Prints

Styrofoam Texture Prints

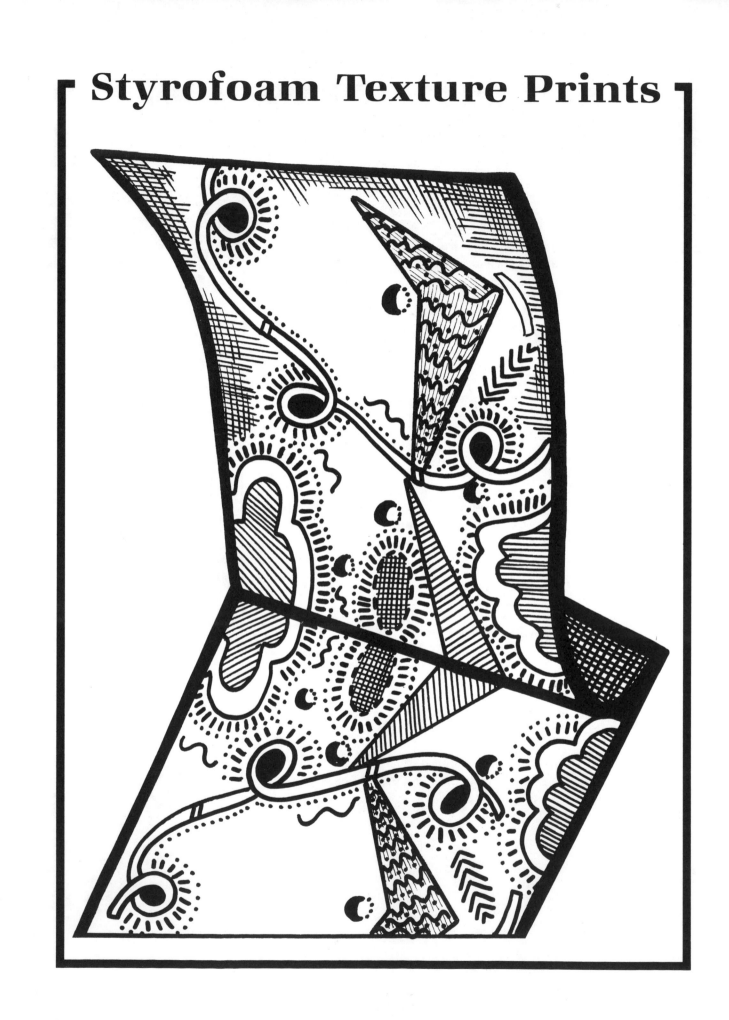

STYROFOAM TEXTURE PRINTS

Materials:

- styrofoam meat trays
- hard textural objects such as keys, gears, screws, combs, shells, and so forth
- scissors
- water-based printing ink
- printing trays
- brayers
- printing paper

First the Egyptians and then the Chinese and Japanese made hand-carved **relief designs** which could be reproduced in numbers. Later, blocks were carved to print textiles in Europe. Children begin life by making a print. A nurse applies some ink to the soles of a baby's feet and the doctor presses them against paper.

Directions:

1. Cut off the edges of the styrofoam tray so that you are left with a flat piece.

2. Using various textural objects, press a design deeply into the styrofoam.
3. As with any composition, try to include some large, some medium, and some small designs.
4. Roll out ink and roll over the design.

5. Lay printing paper on the design and rub the back of the paper with your finger tips.
6. Carefully peel off the print and let dry.

Linoleum Block Prints

LINOLEUM BLOCK PRINTS

Materials:

- 9″ × 12″ manila paper
- 9″ × 12″ unmounted linoleum block
- linoleum cutting tools
- pencil and eraser
- tracing paper
- thin, black markers and thick, black markers
- water-based printing ink
- inking tray
- brayers
- barens
- safety metal bench hook
- absorbent printing paper

Directions:

1. Draw your idea for the linoleum block on the manila paper. Add textural areas to make the drawing more interesting. Shade in certain areas completely. You should end up with one-third of the areas white, one-third of the areas dark, and one-third textured.

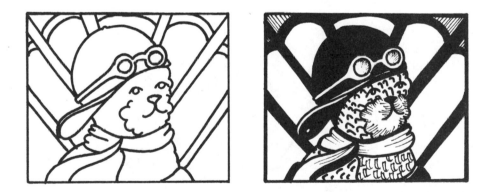

2. Lay carbon paper on your block shiny side down. Lay your drawing over this and attach it with masking tape; trace over the lines, pressing hard with a pencil to transfer the drawing to the block.

3. Trace over all lines, textures, and shaded areas with black markers.

4. Lay the bench hook over the edge of the table and the linoleum block on top.

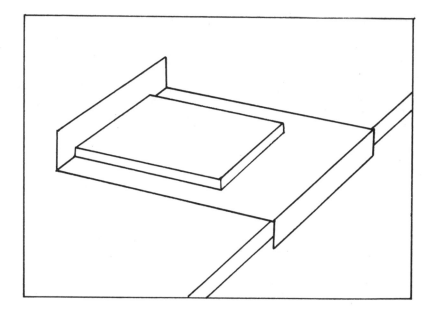

5. Pick up a #2 outlining cutter and hold it so that the handle end is inside your palm and your index finger is on top of the handle.

6. Lay your other hand across the bottom of the block as shown; rest the hand that holds the cutter on top of this hand for safety as shown.

7. Always slice toward the back of the bench hook so that if you slip, you will hit only this. Turn the block when necessary so that you always cut only in this direction.

8. Always keep the hand without the tool resting on the bottom of the block under your other hand for safety.

9. Cut out the outlines of all shapes.

10. Change cutters as necessary to cut out textures and solid areas.

11. Squeeze out ink on a tray and roll over it with a brayer until the tray is evenly covered with ink.

12. Roll ink onto the block quickly.

13. Lay absorbent paper on the block and rub the back of the block with a baren, with the back of a wooden spoon, or with your fingers.

14. Carefully peel off the paper and hang it to dry.

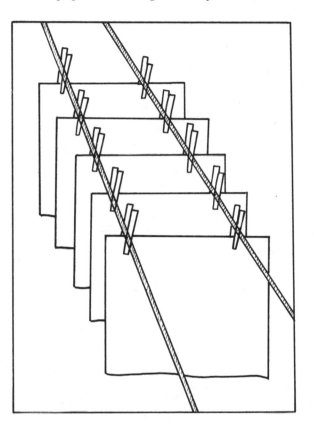

Simple Reduction Print

This technique can be used to produce a multicolor print by cutting away only part of a block, printing it in one color, and letting it dry; then cutting away a little more, printing it in a second color, and letting it dry; and finally cutting away the remainder, printing it, and letting it dry.

Silk-Screen Prints

SILK-SCREEN PRINTS

Materials:

- prepared silk screen
- water-based printing ink
- squeegee
- craft knife

- 2 oaktag pieces the size of the inside of the wood frame
- construction paper
- pencil and eraser

Silk screen is a stencil process using fine cloths that have been painted with an impermeable coating except in areas where color is to be forced through onto paper, cloth, and so forth.

Directions:

1. Draw different "line" shapes on one piece of oaktag to make a stencil. Lines may overlap, as shown.

2. Draw different shapes of varying sizes on the other piece of oaktag to make a stencil. Shapes may overlap.

3. Cut out the lines and shapes with the craft knife.

4. Select a piece of construction paper.

5. Select a color of ink that contrasts with the color of paper you chose.

6. Lift the screen and lay the piece of construction paper on the base piece of wood. Mark the corners of the paper with masking tape so that if you want to make additional prints, you can put each paper in the same position.

7. Next, lay the first stencil on the construction paper.

8. Lay the screen down on the paper and place blobs of ink along one edge of the screen.

9. Using the squeegee, push the ink from one end to the other and back again, forcing the ink through the screen and the holes in the oaktag. Push back and forth several times.

10. Lift the screen and remove the paper to dry.

11. Wash out the screen with running water and a mild liquid soap. Let dry completely. You may even set it in front of a fan.

12. When the first paper is dry, place it under the screen with the second stencil and repeat the printing process with a second color.

13. Let dry.

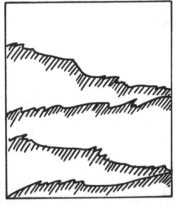

Glue Prints

GLUE PRINTS

Materials:

- white glue in a squeeze bottle
- 12″ × 18″ clipboard
- pencil and eraser
- 12″ × 18″ manila paper
- mimeograph paper or woodblock printing paper
- brayer

Directions:

1. Make a sketch of a simple idea for your print. Make sure your idea fills the space and has one large item that is the most important object in the print.

2. Transfer the drawing to the cardboard.

3. Leave the cap off the container of glue overnight so that it will thicken to a manageable texture.

4. Squeeze the glue along the pencil lines. When dry, you may need a second application along the same lines of the glue to "stand up" high enough in relief to make a print.

5. Set the design aside to dry. It may take several days for the glue to dry completely and to be hard enough to be used for inking and printing.

6. The plate is inked in the same manner as a linoleum cut. An ink-loaded brayer is rolled over the surfaces of the plate and the raised glue lines receive the ink. Some ink will also be retained by background sections. This will produce interesting textured areas in contrast to the more highly defined glue lines.

7. The print is made by carefully placing a sheet of paper over the plate and pressing down lightly on it.

8. Care should be taken so as not to move the paper and thereby blur the print.

9. Mimeograph paper is excellent for printing, but if woodblock printing paper is available, the results will be even finer.

10. Rubbing in a rotating motion with a wooden spoon or flat-surfaced object will produce an interesting print.

11. Many prints can be made from one plate, and the plate itself can be preserved and mounted.

Level 4

Op-Art Weaving expands on previous paper weaving using an uneven weft line to create a design, while *People Weavings* introduces a technique for creating a recognizable form within the weaving.

Op-Art Weaving

Level 5

Textural Weaving explores more advanced weaving techniques such as the rya knot and fringe and the use of positive and negative space in weaving as well as the creation of different weaving patterns.

Textural Weaving

Level 6

Basket Weaving involves weaving a three-dimensional object using reeds as a new media.

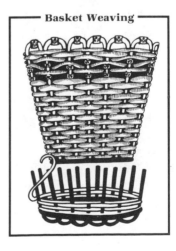

Basket Weaving

Op-Art Weaving

OP-ART WEAVING

Materials:

- 12″ × 18″ black paper
- 12″ × 18″ white paper
- pencil and eraser
- scissors
- ruler

During the sixties, art became concerned with creating a tremendous impact on the eye. Intense, fluorescent color, or black and white together with sharply painted lines and shapes in extra large paintings excited the viewer. **Op-Art** or "Optical Art" was fun! Illusion was often the goal of the painter.

Directions:

1. On the white paper, draw some smooth, curving lines the length of the paper as shown. Cut carefully and smoothly along the lines, and be sure to stop 1″ from each edge.

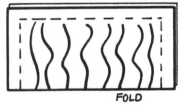

2. Lay the ruler on the end of the black paper the short way and draw a pencil line along the edge. Repeat from left to right across the paper as shown. Cut the strips.

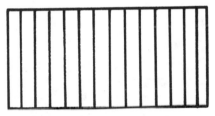

3. Begin weaving the black strips through the white curving lines. Start on the left and weave *over* and *under* across the paper.

4. Alternate the next black strip through the white by going *under* and *over* across the paper.

5. Continue to alternate weaving the black strips completely across the paper until no more strips will fit in, as shown.

6. Glue all the ends of the black strips to the white paper and let dry.

People Weavings

PEOPLE WEAVINGS

Materials:

- looms (wood)
- yarn
- yarn needles
- 12″ × 18″ paper
- pencil and eraser

In every area of the world, **weaving** has been used. The materials that were used—such as grasses and reeds, wool, and animal pelts—were as varied as the climate. Clothing, shelters, baskets, blankets and mats were made.

Directions:

1. Draw a rectangle on paper the size of the loom.

2. Design simple hair, face, arms, skirts or pants, legs, feet, and shoes of a person you want to weave. Label the colors.

3. Remember that warp threads are the vertical threads and that the weft threads run horizontally through the warp.

4. Insert the steel guideposts in each side of the loom to keep the weaving from angling inward. If your loom is handmade and does not come with steel guideposts, you may cut a piece of wire from a coat hanger and trim it to size.

5. Thread your loom by tying around the first notch, then pulling the yarn taut directly across to the notch on the other side, around this notch and back. Continue until you reach the end and wrap your yarn around the last notch and knot.

6. Tie your first color yarn to the end warp and thread through a yarn needle. Continue to weave this color in and out in the areas for this color only.

7. When two colors meet, you must dove-tail them so that both colors wrap around the same warp thread where they meet.

8. Continue working with your other colors until all areas are filled in. Remember to contast light colors next to dark colors so that the different parts of the "person" show up.

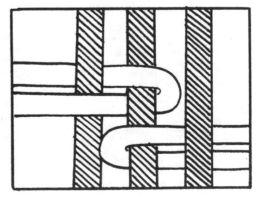

Textural Weaving

TEXTURAL WEAVING

Materials:

- looms
- shuttles
- yarn needles
- yarn
- masking tape

Directions:

1. Remember that warp threads are the vertical threads and that the weft threads run horizontally, weaving through the warp.

2. Insert the steel guideposts in each side of the loom to keep the weaving from angling inward.

3. Thread the loom by tying the first notch, then pulling the yarn tautly across to the notch on the other side, around this notch and back. Continue until you reach the end, wrap around the last notch, and knot.

4. Lay masking tape along each end to keep yarn in the notches.

5. Tie your first color yarn to the end warp and thread through a yarn needle. Continue to weave this color in and out in the areas for this only.

6. When two colors meet, you must dovetail them so that both colors wrap around the same warp thread where they meet, as shown.

7. A rya knot can be included to make a fringe or carpet-looking row or area, as shown. Pull the knot tight and slide it down next to the other weaving. For the next row of rya knots, use one of the warp threads from the last knot above this and from the next wrap use one thread to wrap your knot around.

8. Alternating the threads will make all the knots stay in place better and will also make the finished piece look better.

9. To achieve curved shapes within the weaving, weave through a thread the regular way and then push it into the desired curve and fill in next to it with more lines of yarn until the desired space is filled in.

10. Lines can weave part way across, then turn and come back to achieve desired shapes in certain sections.

11. Empty negative space can be left.

12. A single or double warp cord can be wrapped tightly around and tied to achieve a spiraling effect, as shown.

13. Weaving patterns can change, such as from over one–under one to over two–under three, to achieve a different look. Just remember to keep up the new pattern for several rows before changing, or the pattern will not emerge.

14. Beads can be added by threading them on at any time or by adding them to the warp threads at the beginning.

15. When finished, remove the masking tape and pull the yarn out of the notches.

16. Fringe can be tied to the bottom when finished.

17. The top loops can be laced through with a stick in order to hang your weaving.

Basket Weaving

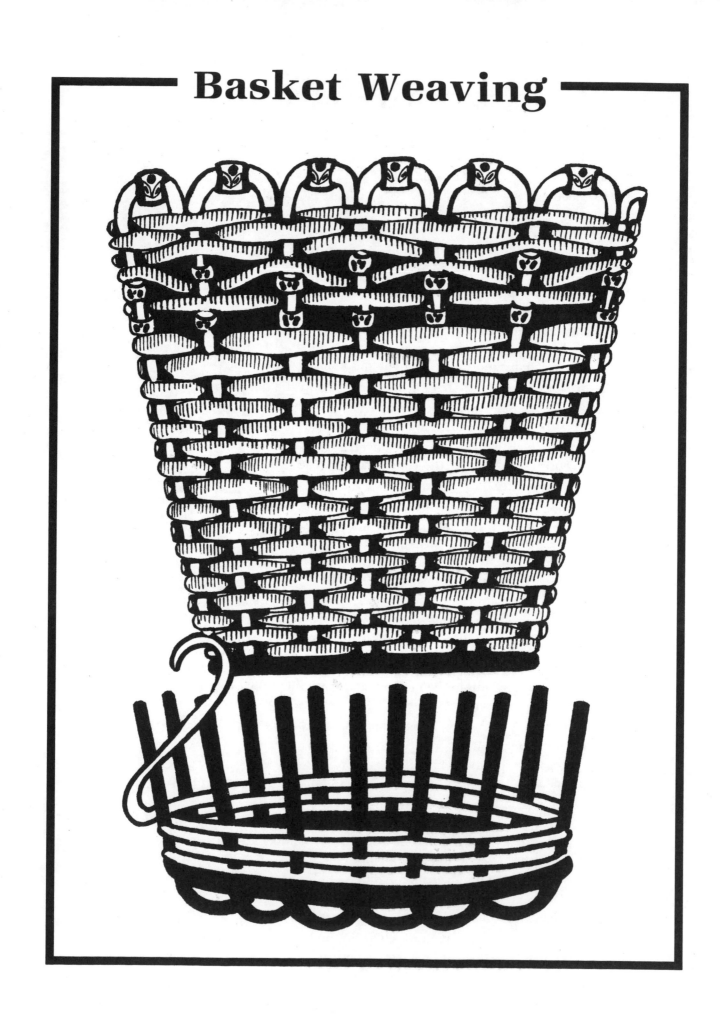

BASKET WEAVING

Materials:

- precut basket base (round or oval) with holes drilled
- #4 reed to be used for spokes
- #2 reed to be used for weaving

Basket weaving has been done for thousands of years. In Egypt, many were found in tombs in the pyramids. At this time, baskets were used functionally—that is, to carry objects. Later, when they began to be painted they started to evolve into something more, and today many are appreciated for their beauty alone. The Indians and the Shakers in America became very skilled in their basket making. Baskets were woven of reeds, grasses, splints, straw, and cord.

Directions:

1. Begin by placing the #4 and the #2 reeds in a container of water to soak. This will take about half an hour, so you may want to prepare this ahead of time.

2. Next, decide how tall you would like your basket to be. Whatever length you choose, add five inches to it. This is to allow extra length for the two parts of the reed which will be folded over.

3. Next, cut the #4 reeds to the desired length, and then insert them into the holes in the basket base. Let the reeds extend 2″ below the base as shown.

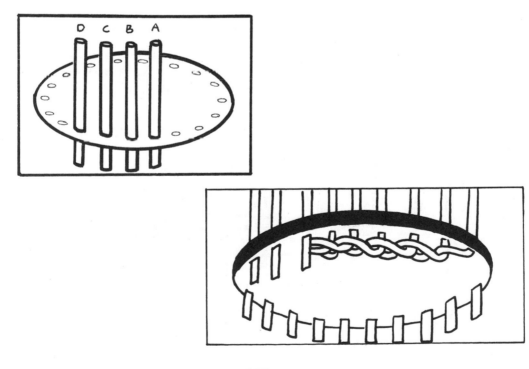

4. Starting with spoke A, weave the part which extends from the base around the outside of spoke B and secure it in front of spoke C. Next, weave spoke B around spoke C and secure it in front of spoke D. Follow the same procedure for the rest of the spokes.

5. Before you begin weaving the thin reed through the spokes, bend the spokes outward so that the sides of your basket will slant. Now you are ready to begin weaving the #2 reed in and out around the spokes. Make sure that the ends of each are inside the basket.

6. When you are finished weaving, you can complete your basket by taking the end of spoke A and looping it over and pushing the end down alongside spoke C. Push the end of spoke B down alongside spoke D. Continue this procedure until the edge is completed.

7. Upon completion, the baskets can be painted or preserved with a coat of shellac. If you wish to add beads, you can slide these onto the desired spokes at any point and then just continue to weave around them.

Level 4

Puppet on a String introduces a simple marionette with further work in costume design, characterization, and sewing. *Papier-Mâché Flu Bugs* reinforces the technique of papier-mâché with a wire armature, while *Fluorocarbon Foam Sculpture* explores carving as a new technique. *Creative Problem Solving* examines architecture using lines, as well as two-dimensional and three-dimensional forms to create fantasy structures for a specific purpose.

Puppet on a String

Level 5

Gnomes involves further three-dimensional construction, while *Milk Jug Masks* gives continued work with characterization using various three-dimensional found objects in a relief form. *Butterfly Batik* introduces "batik" as an art form and also further work with detail. *Robots* involves creating a three-dimensional structure using scrap materials.

Butterfly Batik

Level 6

Balsa Wood Houses includes more advanced architectural concepts, presents a scale-plan drawing and further use with scrap materials, and the introduction of balsa wood. *Marionettes* involves more advanced marionettes and controls along with more advanced costume design and characterization. *Sand Casting* provides more advanced incised designing and the introduction of the new technique of sand casting. *Clone Soft Sculpture* continues sewing and costume design as well as presenting the technique of making dolls. *Creativity Kits* illustrates how unrelated scrap objects can be combined to create an art form. *Animation* introduces the use of a movie camera and the technique "animation," while *Zodiac Banners* presents the art form of banners and reinforces sewing techniques.

Animation

Puppet on a String

PUPPET ON A STRING

Materials:

- one pipe cleaner
- spools
- cardboard
- fabric
- sharp scissors
- lattice
- string
- paint and brush
- plaster-impregnated gauze
- small paper clips
- newspaper
- oaktag
- masking tape
- thin, black marker
- yarn, feathers, and so forth
- staples

In such countries as Indonesia, Formosa, China, and Japan, the wide use of **puppets** goes back as far as the beginnings of recorded history. Puppets have been found in the ancient graves of Greece. In our own country, the Indians used puppets in religious ceremonies long before the coming of the first European settlers. The Hindus once held a belief that each of their sacred puppets had lived with the gods.

Directions:

1. Crumple a single sheet of newspaper into a ball shape and put tape around the ball so that it will hold its shape.
2. Tape the head to a spool, which forms its neck.
3. Use oaktag or newspaper to add features to the head, such as hats and beaks.
4. Twist a pipe cleaner into a small loop and tape it to the top of the head.
5. Layer and overlap gauze over the head and features, halfway down the neck and around the pipe cleaner loop to hold securely. Let dry.
6. Paint the head. Let dry.
7. Lay out on appropriate piece of fabric and draw the body somewhat like the shape shown.

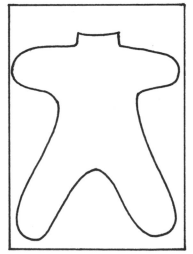

151

8. Cut out two pieces as patterns and sew them together using an overhand stitch close to the edge and leave openings at the neck, ends of the arms and ends of the legs.

9. Turn the costume.

10. Glue the neck spool into the neck opening of the costume and wrap with a piece of masking tape until dry.

11. Draw and cut out hand shapes from thin cardboard with an extension as shown. No more than four fingers are needed.

12. Draw and cut foot shapes from thin cardboard and glue onto a spool as shown.

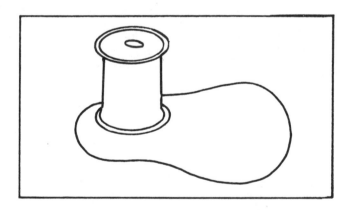

13. Layer gauze over the hands and feet halfway up the spool. Let dry.

14. Glue the hand extension and foot spool into the fabric openings and wrap masking tape around them until they dry.

15. Add yarn, feathers, and other details.

16. Cardboard wings for birds can replace the arms.

17. Cut two pieces of lattice, each 6″ long. Cross the pieces, glue, and tape until dry.

18. Tie 2′ pieces of string at the end of each piece of lattice, glue, and tape in place.
19. Tie strings to the head pipe cleaner loop, wrists, and ankles as shown. Shorten the strings as necessary to achieve a straight string from the control to the puppet in each area.

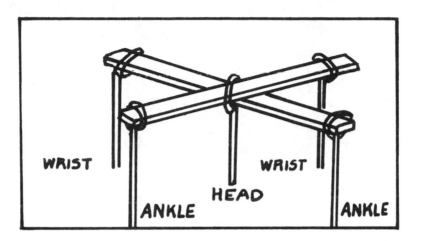

Papier-Mâché Flu Bugs

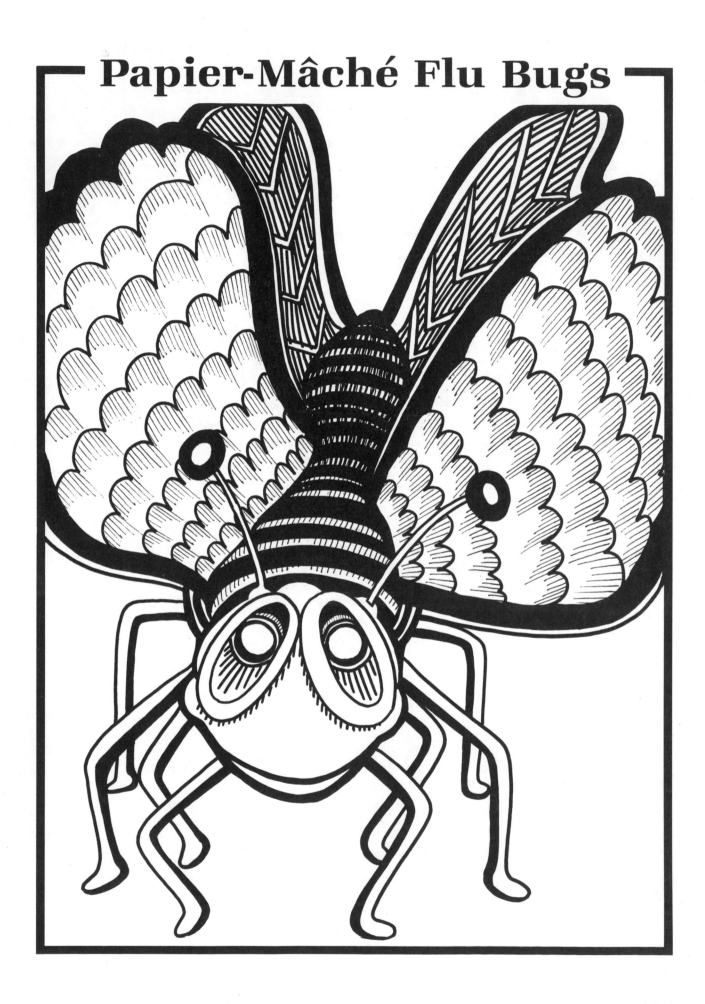

PAPIER-MÂCHÉ FLU BUGS

Materials:

- flexible aluminum wire
- newspaper
- masking tape
- wire cutter
- tempera and brush
- tissue paper
- scissors
- 12″ × 18″ paper
- pencil and eraser
- acrylic polymer medium
- plaster-impregnated gauze

Papier-mâché is a substance made of pulped paper or paper mixed with glue or layers of paper glued and pressed together, which are molded when moist and which become hard and strong when dry. The Chinese were the first to use this method, and they used it to create strong furniture.

Directions:

1. Draw your idea of a horrible flu bug. Make it menacing.
2. Lay out two sheets of newspaper on top of each other and fold them in half. Fold the paper in half again.
3. Cut a piece of wire about 3″ longer than the length of the paper and lay it inside the paper. Roll the wire up inside the paper.
4. Bend another piece of wire in one of the shapes shown for one wing.
5. Do the same for the other wing.
6. Roll up newspaper to make a body, as shown.
7. Attach wings onto the body with tape.
8. Wings can be your idea or like the one shown.
9. The body an be bent, as shown.
10. Wad a piece of newspaper into a ball and tape to hold.
11. Part of the head can be pushed in to form a mouth and teeth, and a tongue can be added.
12. Tape a pipe cleaner—cut in half—onto the head for antennae.
13. Bulging eyes, other features, bumps on the body, and wings can be added with a wad of newspaper or oaktag cut in a desired shape.
14. Pipe cleaner legs can also be added.
15. The wings can be made of flat sheets of newspaper cut to fit, laid on the frame, and taped to hold.
16. Cover the entire form, except for the antennae, with plaster-impregnated gauze. Let dry.
17. Paint with tempera, including patterns and designs.
18. Coat with a layer of acrylic polymer medium.

Fluorocarbon Foam Sculpture

FLUOROCARBON FOAM SCULPTURE

Materials:

- fluorocarbon foam blocks
- simple carving tools like spoons, popsicle sticks, clay modeling tools
- shallow box (to collect the carvings)
- 12″ × 18″ manila paper
- pencil and eraser
- ruler
- scissors

Sculpture is an art form that is three-dimensional. It has height, width, and depth. When making sculpture, the artist must remember to look at all sides while working because they are all important.

Directions:

1. Make a drawing on a piece of 12″ × 18″ manila paper of what you want to carve.
2. Measure the sides of the block and cut three papers to these sizes.
3. Transfer this preliminary drawing to the three papers with a different view on each—front, side, and back, as shown.

4. Make sure each drawing touches all edges of the paper. Cut out each.
5. Lay drawing on its appropriate side and draw around it into the foam blocks.
6. Place the block in a box to do the carving.
7. Next, round out the forms by turning the block constantly as you go.
8. Incise the edge of shapes to emphasize parts or features you want to bring out.
9. First use rough and then medium sandpaper to finish.

Creative Problem Solving

CREATIVE PROBLEM SOLVING

Materials:

- toothpicks
- egg cartons
- styrofoam sheets
- scissors
- masking tape
- glue
- slides or photos of various architecture

To be **creative** means to use one's own original ideas or imagination.

Directions:

1. Look at slides or photos of various architecture, including fantasy architecture from space and adventure movies or stories.
2. Architectural design is made up of line, two-dimensional, and three-dimensional forms.
3. Construct three buildings, each using only one of the above elements as its basis.
4. In addition, make one of each of these buildings that is appropriate for the following movies:
   - a story about fairies and angels who live in a beautiful place.
   - a story about evil creatures on another planet who capture all who land on their planet.
   - a story about some strong, friendly giants who welcome all who enter their kingdom.

Gnomes

GNOMES

Materials:

- empty fruit juice can
- cardboard cone
- scissors
- felt
- fiberfill stuffing, cotton, or white fur

- medium-sized styrofoam ball
- cardboard
- pom-pom
- masking tape
- white glue

A **gnome** is one of a species of small beings fabled to inhabit the interior of the earth and to act as guardian of its treasures. It is usually thought of as a shriveled little old man or a troll.

Directions:

1. Take one empty fruit juice can and attach a styrofoam ball to the top with glue.

2. Next, model the face by using thin strips of newspaper dipped in watered-down, white glue.

3. A beard can be made by attaching fiberfill or cotton to the face with white glue. You can also use some for eyebrows or for hair.

4. Next, attach a cone (the cardboard type used to support spools of yarn are an ideal size) or create one from construction paper by cutting out a shape like this. Twist it into a cone and glue the seam.

5. Next, paint the face and cut out felt eyes and cheeks. If so desired, a pom-pom can be used for a nose.

6. The next step is to cover the can with felt to create the clothing. Felt-covered cardboard feet can be taped to the bottom of the can. Extended arms can be added by piercing the sides of the can and running a pipe cleaner through the center, which can later be covered with felt.

Milk Jug Masks

MILK JUG MASKS

Materials:

- empty, plastic gallon container (milk, bleach, and so forth)
- plaster-impregnated gauze
- old scissors
- large plastic bowls
- tempera paint and brushes
- junk items, such as cardboard tubes, egg cartons, cans, feathers, oatmeal box, salt box, toothpaste box
- masking tape
- slides or photos of historical masks

Directions:

1. View slides or photos of historical masks.
2. Cut the plastic container in half so that the handle will become the base for the nose on your mask. (See the illustration.) Cut off the bottom of the container so that you are left with a curved, face-size piece for the mask.
3. Attach various scrap items to your mask with masking tape to create eyes, nose, mouth, ears, eyebrows, teeth, cheeks, hat, or whatever is desired. Make sure that the item stands out far enough in relief so that even when it is covered with plaster-impregnated gauze, the item is still prominent.
4. Scrap objects can be cut in various ways to change their shape.
5. Eyes can be cut through the bottle with a craft knife, if desired.
6. Cut the gauze with old scissors, then dip the gauze into plastic bowls of warm water. Next, layer the gauze in an overlapping fashion to cover all the features and plastic of the bottle that will be the face. No gauze should cover the back of the mask.
7. Try to make the layering as smooth as possible. Rub the gauze with your fingers to smooth the surface and release plaster to fill in the holes in the gauze.
8. After drying, tempera can be used to add color.
9. Feathers, fake fur, yarn, pipe cleaners, raffia, and so forth may also be added.
10. After large painted areas are completed and dried, patterns can be added with a smaller brush in contrasting colors.
11. When dry, scissors can be used to cut out the back and bottom and to make holes in each side to wear the mask or to hang it using string.

Butterfly Batik

BUTTERFLY BATIK

Materials:

- washed, bleached muslin
- pencil and eraser
- water-soluble, bottled wax medium
- stiff, narrow brushes
- cold-water dyes
- brushes

- 12" × 16" paper
- vinegar
- plastic bowls
- newspaper
- an iron
- cold water

Batik is an Indonesian word which describes a form of resist printing obtained when hot wax, an effective resistant to dye, is applied to the fabric. Fine patterns are often made by using a tjanting, a tool for applying hot wax. When the fabric is dyed, only the unwaxed areas of the cloth take the color. Dyeing is carried out in cool water to prevent the wax from melting.

Directions:

1. Draw a simple butterfly shape to fill the paper.
2. Add simple designs in one wing. Repeat the same designs in reverse, on the opposite wing.
3. Copy the drawing on the muslin in a light pencil line.
4. Trace over the lines with the wax solution to which you have mixed enough water so that it can be easily applied, yet it can penetrate and cover the cloth. Let dry.
5. Mix the cold-water dyes in plastic bowls.
6. Using one color for the background and many colors for the inside of the butterfly, brush on the dyes.
7. Let dry.
8. Place the muslin on a thick pad of newspaper with one piece of newsprint on top.
9. Iron over the newsprint and keep changing to a new sheet of the newsprint until all the wax is gone.
10. Wax over the entire cloth with a wide brush.
11. Let dry completely and crinkle the cloth into a ball.
12. Lay flat and paint a strong solution of black dye over the entire cloth.
13. Again, iron out the wax.
14. Finish with a cold-water bath with vinegar to fix the dye and let dry.

Copper Foil Jewelry

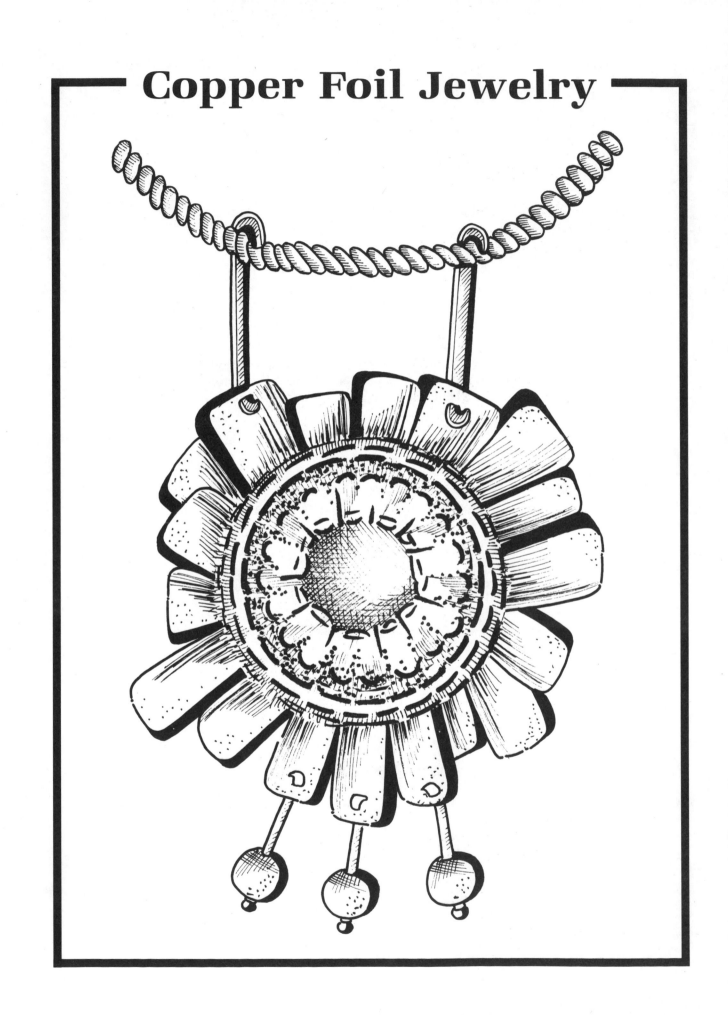

COPPER FOIL JEWELRY

Materials:

- paper and pencil
- 36 gauge copper
- scissors
- craft knives
- metal shears
- needle-nose pliers
- 14, 16, or 18 gauge copper wire or galvanized iron wire (stovepipe)
- rawhide strings
- various found objects for stamping
- wooden stick
- beads, twigs, stone, leather

- jeweler's findings (pin backs, clips, links and catches)
- epoxy
- wire cutters
- ball-pin hammer
- steel block
- liver of sulphur
- fine-grade steel wool
- candle in a secure holder
- acrylics
- slides or photos of jewelry

Directions:

1. View slides or photos of historical and contemporary jewelry.

2. View slides of macrocosmic sections of objects from nature and use the repetition you see to draw pencil designs or preliminary sketches for your finished jewelry. Simplify the basic shapes of birds, fish, and animals.

3. Cut your basic shape or shapes out of the copper with the metal shears.

4. Think of ways you can shape the metal to create interest. You might: (1) cut an opening within a shape; (2) cut a second shape to glue on top of the first shape;

(3) cut a shape and texture the surface by hammering (use a ball-pin hammer and steel block).

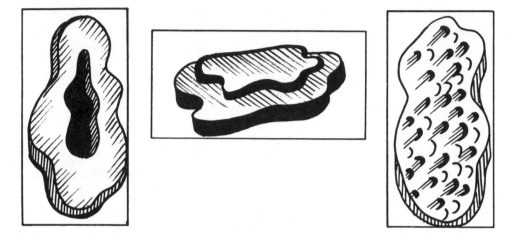

5. Design each shape by the repoussé technique on the metal and connect with rings where necesasry.

6. Cut a piece of wire between 12″ and 18″ long and coil it around a pencil or a small dowel. After removing it from the pencil, stretch it. Coil another piece of wire (similar to the way a rope would be coiled) flat on a table. Pull it out from the center.

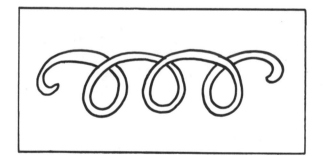

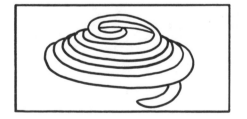

7. Think of how you can convert forms such as these into jewelry. Try other methods for coiling, bending, and twisting wire.

8. How could a series of similarly coiled wire forms be combined into a necklace? Would colorful beads or chunks of stone enhance the design?

9. Flatten a piece of 16 gauge copper wire by hammering it on the steel block. Could you coil this or part of it for your design?

10. If you plan to develop an opening (negative space) within the metal shape, drill a hole at that point, insert scissors and cut away with the points.

11. Metal pieces or jeweler's findings may be joined with epoxy.

12. Remember, the copper foil can be easily cut with scissors, or torn, rolled, folded, or crumpled.

13. Pieces can be joined by rawhide lacing or wire.

14. You can use the repoussé technique of burnishing with a wooden spoon or stick and/or stamping with any hard object. Texture rubbings can be added for surface texture.

15. Outside edges may be folded over and burnished to provide a more rigid and less fragile piece.

16. A patina is achieved by submerging or brushing a solution of liver of sulphur on the surface, then polishing with a fine grade of steel wool to highlight the raised surface.

17. Heat applied to the foil will give a range of varying colors from red to yellow to green and blue. Test on a scrap piece first by holding over a candle.

18. Subtle colors of acrylics painted on the foil and wiped off immediately will give an interesting accent.

Robots

ROBOTS

Materials:

- boxes of all shapes and sizes
- scrap machine parts
- foil
- glue
- paint and brushes
- masking tape
- lights, pipes, hoses, wire
- aluminum foil

Directions:

1. (a) Decide upon a task or tasks you want your robot to perform. How will you simulate this?

   (b) Assemble boxes by gluing and holding them in place with masking tape as they dry. These will form the basic body shape of your robot.

2. Add various scrap materials to construct arms and legs or wheels so the robot can stand or move.

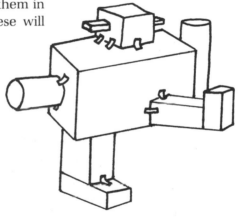

3. Add lights if desired.

4. Add slots for questions, or knobs, or dials.

5. You might cut a hole to expose "machine parts"—which you have glued or wired inside the robot's body.

6. When the construction is complete, paint or cover parts with aluminum foil.

7. You should include a set of directions in order to show how your robot will perform his or her assigned task.

Balsa Wood Houses

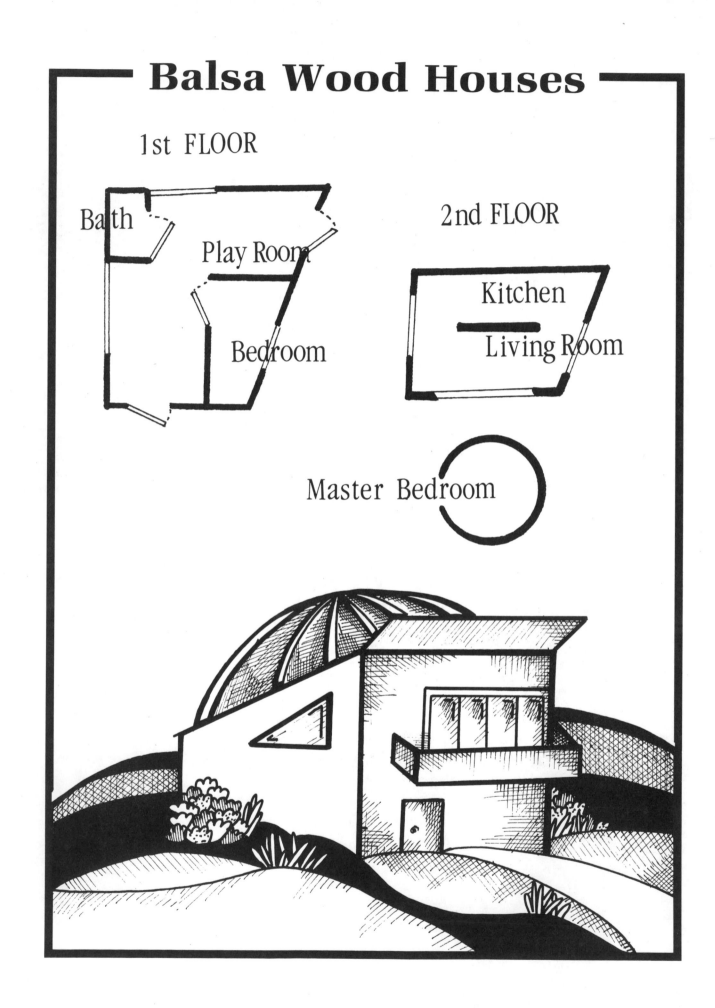

BALSA WOOD HOUSES

Materials:

- pencil and eraser
- 12″ × 18″ paper
- balsa wood and craft knife
- water soluable wood glue
- straight pins
- masking tape
- rulers
- 18″ × 24″ newsboard for base
- dowels, other scrap materials
- plaster-impregnated gauze
- newspaper
- wooden dowels
- stain or paint

Directions:

1. Design and draw the outside elevation and inside floor plan for a vacation house for the year 2000 for a family of four with no more than seven rooms.

 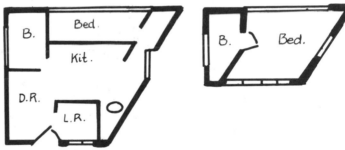

2. Indicate on your paper where you want the house to be built. Take this into consideration when deciding the type of energy to be used in your house, windows, transportation to the house, and so forth.

3. On a board, approximately 18″ × 24″, draw your floor plan.

4. If your house is on irregular ground, build this up first by using crushed wads of newspaper covered with plaster-impregnated gauze.

5. Houses may be on stilts made of wooden dowels.

6. Using balsa wood pieces measuring 3″ × ⅟₁₆″ × 24″, cut the wood so that between 1″ and 1½″ equals one floor wall. Remember to cut out the windows before gluing up the walls on the base.

7. The outside doors should be drawn on and the inside walls cut out.

8. All outside walls should be constructed before the inside walls.

9. The roof should be constructed so that at least part of it can be removed to view the inside of the house.

10. Other scrap materials, such as the bottoms of two-liter soda bottles for skylights and other effects such as acetate for "glass" can be used.

11. When complete, stain or paint your house.

12. Trees or bushes from hobby train stores can be glued on the board, as can sand for beaches, fake grass, and painted lakes or oceans.

13. Possible ideas could be a house on an island, one underwater, one underground, heliports on roofs, computer rooms, robot servants, and so forth.

Marionettes

MARIONETTES

Materials:

- masking tape
- plaster gauze
- empty plastic soda bottle (two-liter)
- craft knife
- muslin
- 1″ wood for feet
- ⅜″ dowel
- cardboard
- felt, material, yarn
- tongue depressor, lattice strips
- screw eyes
- nylon fishing line
- fiberfill stuffing
- newspaper, cardboard

Directions:

1. Sketch your favorite character.
2. Wrap single sheets of newspaper over each other to form a ball and fasten with tape to the top of the bottle. Add features to your head with cardboard or rolled newspaper.
3. Cut four holes in the bottle for arms and legs.

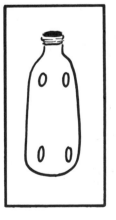

4. Smoothly cover the head and neck with plaster-saturated gauze. Overlap the gauze onto the bottle in order to secure the head.
5. Sew ⅝″ seam on two pieces of muslin which have been cut 3″ × 20″ to be used as arms and legs. Turn the inside out.

6. Push the muslin pieces through the holes and stuff with fiberfill; tie, as shown, at the joints.

7. Cut two wooden feet 1″ × 2½″ and drill a hole in each so that you can insert a ⅜″ × 3″ dowel into each. Secure these with white glue.

8. Cut out two cardboard hands and then cover each with felt. When they are dry, glue one inside each arm.

9. Paint the head, arms, legs, feet and hands if you wish. Add yarn or fake fur for hair.

10. Use felt or other materials to construct a costume if one is needed. Your costume can be sewn or glued together.

11. Next, construct your controls using strips of lattice and a tongue depressor. If possible, drill holes where shown. Overlap strips of wood and then glue them together.

12. The last step is stringing, and this requires that a screw eye be hammered into the head so that the marionette can hang from the controls. Next, use a needle and fishing twine to join the knees and hands to the controls, as shown.

Sand Casting

SAND CASTING

Materials:

- aluminum pie or baking tin
- plaster of paris
- variety of interesting large objects and tools, such as shells, gears, wheels, kitchen gadgets, and sticks
- plastic bucket
- pipe cleaner

Directions:

1. Pack clean, moist sand in a pie or baking tin.
2. Impress a design or push objects into the sand and lift out to leave an impression.

3. With your hands, mix plaster of paris into a plastic bucket which already has some water in it by slowly adding some of the plaster powder until the mixture has the consistency of heavy cream.
4. Pour the plaster over the sand and into the impressions. Embed a bent pipe cleaner to use as a hanger.
5. When the plaster is fully set, loosen by gently bending the aluminum pan.
6. Brush off loose sand with a soft brush, but leave the sandy surface which is embedded in the plaster.
7. Sand casting will not reproduce the minute details that a clay casting will.
8. Quick, bold designs work best.

Clone Soft Sculpture

CLONE SOFT SCULPTURE

Materials:

- felt
- fabric
- yarn
- sharp scissors
- craft or fabric glue
- polyester fiberfill
- thread and needle
- straight pins
- nylons and socks
- costume jewelry
- wigs
- hairpieces
- furs
- sequins
- buttons
- collars and ties
- artificial flowers
- glasses
- 18″ × 24″ manila paper

A **clone** is the exact duplicate of another living thing.

Directions:

1. Make a list of all your personality traits. Include a list of things you love, things you dislike, what makes you excited or happy, what makes you sad, what hobbies you have, and what sports you like.
2. On a piece of 18″ × 24″ manila paper, draw a simple human figure, perhaps in a position you often take.
3. Pin this to a folded piece of felt.
4. Sew a blanket stitch all of the way around the figure.
5. There are also three other stuffed people shapes you could make: (1) The single-shape doll contains head, arms, trunk and legs in one shape; parts are not added separately. (2) The arch-shape doll contains the head and the body; the arms and legs are added separately. (3) The stocking doll is created from old nylons, stuffed, stitched and formed into a head, body, arms, and legs.

6. For the single-shape and arch-shape doll, the directions include making a paper pattern, pinning it to doubled cloth, cutting it out, and sewing the two parts together. Leave a hole for the stuffing. The stocking doll requires that you wrap and tie a section of nylon stocking around a head-shaped ball of stuffing.

7. Your pattern should not be too skinny or too complicated, or it will be impossible to sew and stuff. With the arch-shape doll, the pattern is no problem—it's just a big arch shape. The stocking doll needs no pattern at all.

8. Remember to place the pattern on the edge of the fabric, not in the center.

9. Pin the fronts and backs. Choose the running stitch, overcast, or blanket stitch. See the illustration below.

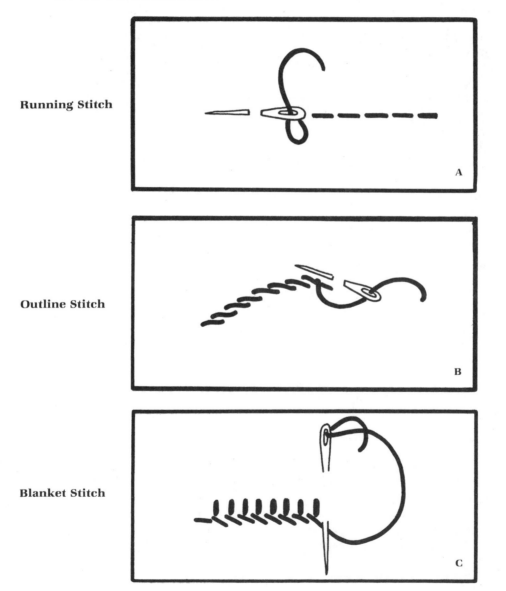

Running Stitch A

Outline Stitch B

Blanket Stitch C

10. Stitch around the outside edge of your doll and remember to leave an opening for the stuffing.

11. If you have used a running stitch, you may wish to turn your doll inside out after stitching.

12. With a stocking doll, once you have formed and tied a stocking head, begin a nose by making small stitches through the nylon and the stuffing and pulling them tight.

13. Experiment with ways to form eyes, lips, and cheeks with a stocking doll. Stitch arms, legs, and bodies together.

14. Clothes can be sewn or glued onto the doll.

15. Optional finishing touches such as hair, eyelashes, and fingernails are glued to the outside of the clone.

16. Items may be made and added to the clone to make them look more like you, that is, a book, a baseball bat, a science beaker, riding boots, and so forth.

17. Remember you are making a clone—an exact duplicate of you—so *always* keep this in mind when forming the features, the color of the hair and style, the type of clothes and props.

Creativity Kits

CREATIVITY KITS

Materials:

- 2 pipe cleaners
- 2 popsicle sticks
- 2 paper clips
- 2 plastic straws
- 2 toothpicks
- 2 brass paper fasteners
- 2 sheets colored or white paper, 9″ × 12″
- 1 sheet oaktag, 9″ × 12″
- scissors
- glue
- pencil and eraser
- markers
- string
- stapler

Directions:

1. Using *all* of the materials given above, construct a three-dimensional recognizable object. Try to stretch your imagination to make something really different.

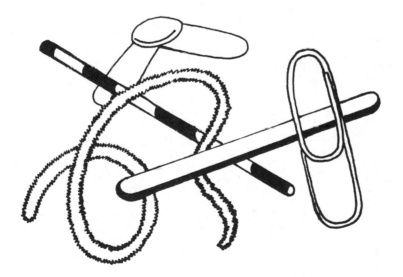

2. You may also use standard art supplies, such as scissors, glue, pencil, and eraser.
3. Try to avoid the obvious.

Animation

ANIMATION

Materials

- super 8 mm camera with a macrozoom lens and a single frame adjustment (a video camera would be an alternative choice)
- extra long cable release
- editor and splicer (optional)
- splicing tapes
- reels
- plasticene
- pencil and eraser
- paint and brushes and glue
- pieces of butcher paper, 18″ × 24″
- 3 or 4 pieces of illustration board, 18″ × 24″
- 2 reflector floodlights of 300 watts and clamps or poles in porcelain sockets
- cassette recorder

Directions:

1. Write an original short story using characters that are inventive and creative. Include conversation and sound effects.
2. Stress exaggerated action and descriptive words.
3. Draw and paint scenery on butcher paper and glue it onto a piece of illustration board.
4. Mold your characters and props out of plasticene and remember to keep them in proportion to an area that measures 18″ × 24″.
5. Different heads can be made for the characters to interchange so that different facial expressions can be shown.
6. Colors of characters must be in contrast to the scenery so that they can be seen.
7. Use a simple frame-cable release to shoot two frames, then move an arm, leg, and/or head of your character *slightly*. Shoot another two frames or clicks with the cable release.
8. Shoot every scene in sequence to avoid as much editing and splicing as possible. (Directions are easy and come with the editor.)
9. Remember that 24 frames = 1 second of the movie—so your movements or changes between every two frames must be small.
10. Two frames per move will give you fairly smooth action when the film is projected.
11. You can write conversation on cardboard and insert these in between the action, or you can view the film when it is finished and tape the voices and sound effects on a cassette.

Zodiac Banners

ZODIAC BANNERS

Materials:

- butcher paper
- drawing paper
- pencil and eraser
- sharp scissors
- felt and fabric
- fabric or craft glue
- markers
- burlap

- large tapestry needles
- rug, knitting, brill yarns
- embroidery paint and brushes
- various found objects including mirrors, sequins, lace, rick-rack, braid, trims, roving, and so forth
- wooden dowels

Directions:

1. Banners came into use in the Middle Ages and were carried into battles to show certain groups or rulers. Later, business people used them in front of their shops for advertising. Banners are used today to decorate, advertise, and identify.

2. Using the zodiac symbol for your birth month, draw an idea for a banner and use the symbol as the central idea. Include objects around it showing something about you, your characteristics, and the things you enjoy. Perhaps you could show a turtle because everything you do, you do slowly and carefully. Or, you could show a book because you love to read.

3. You might include your favorite foods.

4. Various objects should be organized in groups or sections and separated by lines, designs, or colors into certain areas.

5. When your sketch is organized, transfer it to butcher paper and outline objects in black marker.

6. Select a color of burlap and cut out the desired size.

7. Edges should be either fringed or trimmed with ready-made fringe.

8. Tops should be turned over and stitched down to allow for the dowel sticks.

9. Roving should be braided and attached to each end of the stick.

10. Use objects cut from the butcher paper to trace around the felt or fabric. Cut the objects out and glue them into place.

11. Large needles and yarns can be used to add stitchery where desired.

12. A decorative quality can be achieved by using junk jewelry, feathers, mirrors, plastic eyes, sticks, and buttons.

13. Embroidery paint can be used for smaller details and outlines.